"EXTRAORDINARY . . . INTENSE, MOVING, DRAMATIC"

San Francisco Chronicle & Examiner

"Wonderful. . . . **The best living American novelist is also a man of brains.** Veteran reader, seasoned talker, Saul Bellow handles ideas with the same juggling ease that he tells stories. . . . Bellow delights in the liveliness, the gallantry of Israeli life." Irving Howe, *The New York Times*

"**The most precise reading I know of the psychological climate in Israel today.**" Peter S. Prescott, *Newsweek*

"It is not often that a book even distantly connected with Israel will make the reader laugh out loud with pleasure at what **Bellow surely found the least boring place on earth.**" Teddy Kollek (Mayor of Jerusalem), *The New Republic*

(continued . . .)

"A LITERARY CORNUCOPIA"

The Washington Post.

Other Avon Books by
Saul Bellow

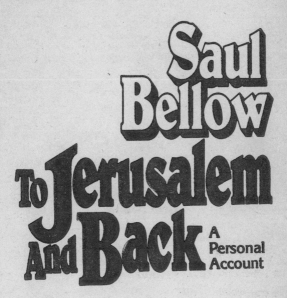

Saul Bellow

To Jerusalem And Back

A Personal Account

AVON
PUBLISHERS OF BARD, CAMELOT AND DISCUS BOOKS·

A substantial part of this book appeared originally in *The New Yorker*.

Acknowledgment for material quoted is made to the following: Cornell University Press, for material from *Aleksander Blok: The Journey to Italy* by Lucy Vogel. Copyright © 1973 by Cornell University. Used by permission of Cornell University Press.

The New York Times, for material from "Open Letter to an Israeli Friend" by Joseph Alsop. © 1975 by The New York Times Company. Reprinted by permission.

Oxford University Press, for material from *The Arab Cold War* by Malcolm Kerr (3rd ed. 1971). © Oxford University Press 1971. Reprinted by permission of Oxford University Press.

The portrait of Saul Bellow on the front cover is from a copyrighted photograph by Jill Krementz.

AVON BOOKS
A division of
The Hearst Corporation
959 Eighth Avenue
New York, New York 10019

Copyright © Saul Bellow, 1976
Published by arrangement with The Viking Press.
Library of Congress Catalog Card Number: 76-42198
ISBN: 0-380-01676-1

First Avon Printing, July, 1977

AVON TRADEMARK REG. U.S. PAT. OFF. AND IN
OTHER COUNTRIES, MARCA REGISTRADA,
HECHO EN U.S.A.

Printed in the U.S.A.

To Jerusalem And Back

SECURITY measures are strict on flights to Israel, the bags are searched, the men are frisked, and the women have an electronic hoop passed over them, fore and aft. Then hand luggage is opened. No one is very patient. Visibility in the queue is poor because of the many Hasidim with their broad hats and beards and side-locks and dangling fringes who have descended on Heathrow and are far too restless to wait in line but rush in and out, gesticulating, exclaiming. The corridors are jumping with them. Some two hundred Hasidim are flying to Israel to attend the circumcision of the firstborn son of their spiritual leader, the Belzer Rabbi. Entering the 747, my wife, Alexandra, and I are enfiladed by eyes that lie dark in hairy ambush. To me there is nothing foreign in these hats, sidelocks, and fringes. It is my childhood revisited. At the age of six, I myself wore a tallith katan, or scapular, under my shirt, only mine was a scrap of green calico print, whereas theirs are white linen. God instructed Moses to speak to the children of Israel and to "bid them that they make them fringes in the borders of their garments." So they are still wearing them some four thousand years later. We find our seats, two in a row of three, toward the rear of the aircraft. The third is occupied by a young Hasid, highly excited, who is staring at me.

"Do you speak Yiddish?" he says.

"Yes, certainly."

"I cannot be next to your wife. Please sit between us. Be so good," he says.

1

"Of course."

I take the middle seat, which I dislike, but I am not really put out. Curious, rather. Our Hasid is in his late twenties. He is pimply, his neck is thin, his blue eyes goggle, his underlip extrudes. He does not keep a civilized face. Thoughts and impulses other than civilized fill it—by no means inferior impulses and thoughts. And though he is not permitted to sit beside women unrelated to him or to look at them or to communicate with them in any manner (all of which probably saves him a great deal of trouble), he seems a good-hearted young man and he is visibly enjoying himself. All the Hasidim are vividly enjoying themselves, dodging through the aisles, visiting chattering standing impatiently in the long lavatory lines, amiable, busy as geese. They pay no attention to signs. Don't they understand English? The stewardesses are furious with them. I ask one of the hostesses when I may expect to receive a drink and she cries out in irritation, "Back to your seat!" She says this in so ringing a voice that I retreat. Not so the merry-minded Hasidim, exulting everywhere. The orders given by these young gentile uniformed females are nothing to them. To them they are merely attendants, exotic *bediener,* all but bodyless.

Anticipating a difficulty, I ask the stewardess to serve me a kosher lunch. "I can't do that, we haven't enough for *them,*" she says. "We weren't prepared." Her big British eyes are affronted and her bosom has risen with indignation. "We've got to go out of our way to Rome for more of their special meals."

Amused, my wife asks why I ordered the kosher lunch. "Because when they bring my chicken dinner this kid with the beard will be in a state," I explain.

And so he is. The British Airways chicken with the chill of death upon it lies before me. But after three hours of security exercises at Heathrow I am hungry. The young Hasid recoils when the tray is handed to me. He addresses me again in Yiddish. He says, "I must talk to you. You won't be offended?"

"No, I don't think so."

"You may want to give me a slap in the face."

"Why should I?"

"You *are* a Jew. You must be a Jew, we are speaking Yiddish. How can you eat—*that*!"

"It looks awful, doesn't it?"

"You mustn't touch it. My womenfolk packed kosher-beef sandwiches for me. Is your wife Jewish?"

Here I'm obliged to lie. Alexandra is Rumanian. But I can't give him too many shocks at once, and I say, "She has not had a Jewish upbringing."

"She doesn't speak Yiddish?"

"Not a word. But excuse me, I want my lunch."

"Will you eat some of my kosher food instead, as a favor?"

"With pleasure."

"Then I will give you a sandwich, but only on one condition. You must never—never—eat *trephena* food again."

"I can't promise you that. You're asking too much. And just for one sandwich."

"I have a duty toward you," he tells me. "Will you listen to a proposition?"

"Of course I will."

"So let us make a deal. I am prepared to pay you. If you will eat nothing but kosher food, for the rest of your life I will send you fifteen dollars a week."

"That's very generous," I say.

"Well, you are a Jew," he says. "I must try to save you."

"How do you earn your living?"

"In a Hasidic sweater factory in New Jersey. We are all Hasidim there. The boss is a Hasid. I came from Israel five years ago to be married in New Jersey. My rabbi is in Jerusalem."

"How is it that you don't know English?"

"What do I need English for? So, I am asking, will you take my fifteen dollars?"

"Kosher food is far more expensive than other kinds,"

I say. "Fifteen dollars isn't nearly enough."

"I can go as far as twenty-five."

"I can't accept such a sacrifice from you."

Shrugging, he gives up and I turn to the twice disagreeable chicken and eat guiltily, my appetite spoiled. The young Hasid opens his prayer book. "He's so fervent," says my wife. "I wonder if he's praying for you." She smiles at my discomfiture.

As soon as the trays are removed, the Hasidim block the aisles with their *Minchah* service, rocking themselves and stretching their necks upward. The bond of common prayer is very strong. This is what has held the Jews together for thousands of years. "I like them," says my wife. "They're so lively, so childlike."

"You might find them a little hard to live with," I tell her. "You'd have to do everything their way, no options given."

"But they're cheerful, and they're warm and natural. I love their costumes. Couldn't you get one of those beautiful hats?"

"I don't know whether they sell them to outsiders."

When the Hasid returns to his seat after prayer, I tell him that my wife, a woman of learning, will be lecturing at the Hebrew University in Jerusalem.

"What is she?"

"A mathematician."

He is puzzled. "What is that?" he asks.

I try to explain.

He says, "This I never heard of. What actually is it they do?"

I am astonished. I knew that he was an innocent but I would never have believed him to be ignorant of such a thing. "So you don't know what mathematicians are. Do you know what a physicist is? Do you recognize the name of Einstein?

"Never. Who is he?"

This is too much for me. Silent, I give his case some thought. Busy-minded people, with their head-culture that touches all surfaces, have heard of Einstein. But do they know what they have heard? A majority do not. These Hasidim choose not to know. By and by I open a a paperback and try to lose myself in mere politics. A dozen Hasidim in the lavatory queue stare down at us.

We land and spill out and go our separate ways. At the baggage carousel I see my youthful Hasid again and we take a final look at each other. In me he sees what deformities the modern age can produce in the seed of Abraham. In him I see a piece of history, an antiquity. It is rather as if Puritans in seventeenth-century dress and observing seventeenth-century customs were to be found still living in Boston or Plymouth. Israel, which receives us impartially, is accustomed to strange arrivals. But then Israel is something else again.

WE are staying in Jerusalem as guests of the
Mishkenot Sha'ananim, the dwellings of se-
renity. Mayor Teddy Kollek, irrepressible organizer of wonderful events (some of them too rich for
my blood), takes us to dinner with one of the Armenian
Archbishops in the Old City. On the rooftop patio of the
opulent apartment are tubs of fragrant flowers. The
moon is nearly full. Below is the church, portions of
which go back to the fourth century. The Archbishop is,
to use an old word, a portly man. His cassock, dark red,
swells with the body. On his breast two ball-point pens
are clipped between the buttons. He has a full youthful
clever face; a black beard, small and tidy. The eyes are
green. Present are Isaac Stern; Alexander Schneider,
formerly of the Budapest String Quartet; Kollek's son,
Amos; two Israeli couples whom I cannot identify; and
the foreign-news editor of *Le Monde,* Michel Tatu. In
the Archbishop's drawing room are golden icons. In illuminated cases are ancient objects. I can seldom get up
much interest in such cases and objects. Middle-aged
Armenians serve drinks and wait on us. They wear extremely loud shirts, blue-green sprigged with red berries,
but they strike me as good fellows and are neat and
nimble about the table. The conversation is quick and
superknowledgeable. In French, in English, in Hebrew,
and occasionally in Russian. (Tatu, who lived for years
in Moscow, chats in Russian with Stern and Schneider.)
The Archbishop, who has himself cooked the eggplant
and the leg of lamb, tells the company his recipes. He

and Kollek discuss seasonings. Schneider recalls a great Armenian musician and teacher (his own teacher) named Dirian Alexanian, editor of Bach's Suites for Cello Unaccompanied and the most intolerant perfectionist—"Just as particular about music as other people are about seasonings. Alexanian said to Pablo Casals after a performance of some of the suites, 'You made three bad mistakes. Terrible.' Casals did not answer. He knew Alexanian was right."

Pale, with black hair in abundance, Tatu is one of those short men who have learned to hold their ground against big ones. He sits with the ease that disguises this sort of tension. His paper is not friendly to Israel. Two or three times I consider whether to mention to him a letter I sent *Le Monde* during the 1973 war about the position being taken by France. I want to ask him why it wasn't printed. But I succeed in suppressing this—a triumph over myself. Besides, Tatu does not have the look of a man whose life is easy and I don't see why I should spoil his Jerusalem dinner for him—in his diary it would probably be entered as "An enchanted evening in Le Proche Orient with an Armenian archbishop." I decide to let him enjoy his dinner. Seeking common ground with my wife (a laudable desire), he tells her that he too is Rumanian by origin. He can safely say this, for his family came to France in the seventeenth century. What is all-important is to be French, or to have been French for a good long time. And French he definitely is. But I can see that the Archbishop gives him bad marks for lighting up after the main course. This is *inculte*. People of real culture do not smoke at dinner tables. You never know whom you have asked to your palace.

The Archbishop is really very handsome, with his full cheeks, his long clear dark-green eyes, and the short strong beard. His church is venerable rich and beautiful. It contains the head of Saint James the brother of John and many relics. The house of Annas, in which Jesus was questioned and struck, is within the compound. The church's manuscript collection is the largest outside

Soviet Armenia. The antique tiles are gorgeous. But all these things are in some way external. We outsiders are not *stable* enough to appreciate them. We inherit our mode of appreciation from the Victorians, from a time of safety and leisure, when dinner guests knew better than to smoke after the main course, when Levantines were Levantines and culture was still culture. But in these days of armored attacks on Yom Kippur, of Vietnams, Watergates, Mansons, Amins, terrorist massacres at Olympic Games, what are illuminated manuscripts, what are masterpieces of wrought iron, what are holy places?

We soon get around to contemporary matters. A call to the telephone; the Archbishop excuses himself in two languages and tells us when he comes back that he has been speaking to one of his Lebanese friends calling from Cyprus or from Greece. He sits down, saying that the influence of Yasir Arafat is evidently weakening and fading. Arafat was unable to complete the classic guerrilla pattern and bring the masses into the struggle. Then someone says that it can't be long now before the Russians write Arafat off. They have undoubtedly recognized their failure in the Arab world and may even be preparing to reopen diplomatic relations with Israel. Most of the dinner guests agree that Russia's internal difficulties are so grave it may have to draw away from Syria. Indeed, it may be forced to retreat from the Middle East and concentrate on its domestic problems. The American grain purchases may not be sufficient. To avoid collapse the Russians may be driven into a war with China. Secretary of State Henry Kissinger has won the Middle Eastern struggle by drawing Egypt into the American camp. He is a genius. The Russians are in disarray, perhaps in retreat.

I have been hearing conversations like this one for half a century. I well remember what intelligent, informed people were saying in the last years of the Weimar Republic, what they told one another in the first days after Hindenburg had brought in Hitler. I recall table talk from the times of Léon Blum and Edouard Daladier. I remember what people said about the Italian adventure in Ethiopia and about the Spanish Civil War and the Battle of Britain. Such intelligent discussion hasn't *always* been wrong. What is wrong with it is that the discussants invariably impart their own intelligence to what they are discussing. Later, historical studies show that what actually happened was devoid of anything like such intelligence. It was absent from Flanders Field and from Versailles, absent when the Ruhr was taken, absent from Teheran, Yalta, Potsdam, absent from British policy at the time of the Palestine Mandate, absent before, during, and after the Holocaust. History and politics are not at all like the notions developed by intelligent, informed people. Tolstoi made this clear in the opening pages of *War and Peace*. In Anna Schérer's salon, the elegant guests are discussing the scandal of Napoleon and the Duc d'Enghien, and Prince Andrei says that after all there is a great difference between Napoleon the Emperor and Napoleon the private person. There are *raisons d'état* and there are private crimes. And the talk goes on. What is still being perpetuated in all civilized discussion is the ritual of civilized discussion itself.

Tatu agrees with the Archbishop about the Russians. So that, as they say in Chicago, is where the smart money is. The Vatican is the next topic and receives similar treatment. Some Armenian prelates have joined us for coffee and take part in the discussion. Someone observes that the Church is a worshiper of success and always follows the majorities. See what it is doing now in the Warsaw Pact countries, it is making deals with the Communists. Should communism sweep Italy, would the Pope move to Jerusalem? Rather, says one of the prelates, he would stay in Rome and become Party secretary. And there we are, Kissinger has entirely wrecked Russia's Middle East policy and the Pope is about to swap the Vatican for the Kremlin. Dessert is served.

In my letter to *Le Monde* I had said that in the French tradition there were two attitudes toward the Jews: a revolutionary attitude which had resulted in their enfranchisement, and an anti-Semitic one. The intellectual leaders of the Enlightenment were decidedly anti-Semitic. I asked which of the two attitudes would prevail in twentieth-century France—the century of the Dreyfus affair and of the Vichy government. The position taken by Foreign Minister Maurice Jobert in the October War of 1973 was that the Palestinian Arabs had a natural and justified desire to "go home." I expressed, politely, the hope that the other attitude, the revolutionary one, would not be abandoned. I made sure that my letter would be delivered. Eugène Ionescu gave the editors one copy of it; another was handed to them by Manès Sperber, the novelist. The letter was never acknowledged.

Since 1973, Le Monde has openly taken the side of the Arabs in their struggle with Israel. It supports terrorists. It is friendlier to Amin than to Rabin. A recent review of the autobiography of a fedayeen speaks of the Israelis as colonialists. On July 3, 1976, before Israel had freed the hostages at Entebbe, the paper observed with some satisfaction that Amin, "the disquieting Marshal," maligned by everyone, had now become the support and the hope of his foolish detractors. Le Monde gloated over this reversal. On July 12, after the raid, Israel was accused of giving comfort to the reactionaries of Rhodesia and South Africa by its demonstration of military superiority and its use of Western arms and techniques, upsetting the balance between poor and rich countries, disturbing the work of men of good will in Paris who were trying to create a new climate and to treat the countries of the Third World as equals and partners. Rhodesians and South Africans, said Le Monde, were toasting the Israelis in champagne. But European approval of the raid would endanger the plans of France for a new international order. On July 4–5, again before the rescue, Le Monde had reported without comment wisecracks made by Amin in a speech at Port Louis. Addressing the OAS, Amin had provoked laughter and applause among the delegates by saying that the hostages

were as comfortable as they could be in the circumstances—surrounded by explosives. "When I left," he
said, laughing, "the hostages wept and begged me to
stay." This broke everybody up.

WE step into the street and my friend David Shahar, whose chest is large, takes a deep breath and advises me to do the same. The air, the very air, is thought-nourishing in Jerusalem, the Sages themselves said so. I am prepared to believe it. I know that it must have special properties. The delicacy of the light also affects me. I look downward toward the Dead Sea, over broken rocks and small houses with bulbous roofs. The color of these is that of the ground itself, and on this strange deadness the melting air presses with an almost human weight. Something intelligible, something metaphysical is communicated by these colors. The universe interprets itself before your eyes in the openness of the rock-jumbled valley ending in dead water. Elsewhere you die and disintegrate. Here you die and mingle. Shahar leads me down from the Mishkenot Sha'ananim, which stands on a slope and faces Mount Zion and the Old City, to the Gai-Hinnom (Gehenna of tradition), where worshipers of Moloch once sacrificed their children. He leads me from the Gai-Hinnom up to an ancient Karaite burial ground, where you can see the mingling for yourself. It acts queerly on my nerves (through the feet, as it were), because I feel that a good part of this dust must be ground out of human bone. I don't know that Jerusalem is geologically older than other places but the dolomite and clay look hoarier than anything I ever saw. Gray and sunken, in the thoughts of Mr. Bloom in Joyce's *Ulysses*. But there is nothing in the brilliant air and the massive white clouds hanging over the crumpled mountains that suggests exhaustion. This atmosphere makes the American commonplace "out of this world" true enough to give your soul a start.

The municipality has turned the Gai-Hinnom into a park. The Wolfson Foundation of London has paid for the planting of gardens, and Arab kids are kicking a soccer ball in the green bottom of the valley. East Jerusalem toughies of fourteen are smoking cigarettes and stiffening their shoulders, practicing the dangerous-loiterer bit as we pass, Shahar lecturing. Shahar is bald, muscular, and his shirt is ornamented with nags, horseshoes, and bridles—a yellow print on dark blue. Amusing, since he's a writer and a thoughtful man, anything but a tout. So we look into ancient tombed caverns and the niches into which corpses once were laid. Now truck fenders are rusting there, the twentieth century adding its crumbling metal to the great Jerusalem dust mixture. You can be absolutely sure, says Shahar, that the Prophet Jeremiah passed this way. Right where we are standing.

I find in Elie Kedourie's *Arabic Political Memoirs* facts unknown to most about American diplomacy in the late forties. Certainly I didn't know them. In the Middle East and probably elsewhere, the United States relied heavily on management consultants and public-relations experts. The American firm of Booz, Allen & Hamilton lent one of its specialists, Miles Copeland by name, to the State Department, where he was in 1955 a member of a group called the Middle East Policy Planning Committee, the main purpose of which was, in his own words, "to work out ways of taking advantage of the friendship which was developing between ourselves and Nasser."*

In 1947 Copeland had been sent to Damascus ("by whom is not stated," Kedourie says) "to make unofficial contact" with Syrian leaders and "to probe for means of persuading them, on their own, to liberalize their political system."

Spreading democracy over the world, the Americans first fought rigged elections in Syria, but the old corruption continued despite all their power and money could do. Frustrated, the Americans decided for the best of reasons, as always, to make a heavier move: "The American Minister at Damascus decided to encourage a military *coup d'état*, so that Syria might enjoy democracy," Kedourie writes. This was not considered particularly bizarre; other American ambassadors and ministers in

The Game of Nations (New York, 1970).

14

the Arab world were entirely in favor of "genuine" revolution to overthrow old landowners, rich crooks, and politicians. "What was wanted was an élite to underpin the rulers, themselves in turn supported and buttressed by a population which presumably understood, approved, and legitimated the aims of such an élite. Whoever knows the Middle East will agree that such a quest was the political equivalent of the search for the philosophical stone."

Failing in Syria, the Americans went to work in Egypt. Kermit Roosevelt of the CIA "met a number of officers who were involved in the conspiracy which led to the *coup d'état* of 22 July, 1952." The Americans wanted the new regime to make the populace literate, to create "a large and stable middle class . . . a sufficient identification of local ideals and values, so that truly indigenous democratic institutions could grow up." Gliding into a new political realm, the Americans arranged for loans to the Egyptian government. They believed that genuine democracy was now on its way. James Eichelberger, a State Department political scientist who had been an account executive for J. Walter Thompson, one of the world's largest advertising and public-relations firms, "was sent to Cairo where he talked with Nasser and his confidants and produced a series of papers identifying the new government's problems and recommending policies to deal with them." One of these papers, written by Eichelberger himself, was translated into Arabic, "commented upon by members of Nasser's staff, translated back into English for Eichelberger's benefit." This document, called "Power Problems of a Revolutionary Government," went back and forth, according to Mr. Copeland, "between English and Arabic until a final version was produced. The final paper was passed off to the outside world as the work of Zakaria Mohieddin, Nasser's most thoughtful (in Western eyes), reasonable deputy, and accepted at face value by intelligence analysts of the State Department, the C.I.A. and, presumably, similar agencies of other governments."

Who would have thought that a former American ac-

count executive could write: "The police should be 'politicized,' and should become, to whatever extent necessary, a partisan paramilitary arm of the revolutionary
government"? This is Leninism, neat, with neither ice
nor bitters. Or, "The nerve center of the whole security
system of a revolutionary state (or of any state) lies in a
secret body, the identity and very existence of which can
be safely known only to the head of the revolutionary
government and to the fewest possible number of other
key leaders." It was Jefferson who said that the tree of
liberty must occasionally be refreshed with the blood of
patriots and tyrants. We must now believe that the same
romantic conviction has been alive somewhere in the
offices of J. Walter Thompson. The United States is,
after all, the *prime* revolutionary country. Or was Mr.
Eichelberger simply an executive with a client to please
and a job to do—a pure professional? Or is there in the
world by now a natural understanding of revolution, of
mass organization, cadres, police rule, and secret executive bodies? This is a shocking suspicion. Of course the
paper written by Mr. Eichelberger and his Egyptian collaborators states that the purpose of the Nasser seizure
of power was "to solve the pressing social and political
problems which made the revolution necessary."

To solve problems, to help, to befriend, to increase
freedom. To strengthen America's position, and at the
same time to do good; to advance the cause of universal
equality; to be the illusionless tough guy on a world
scale; to be a mover and shaker, a shaper of destiny—or
perhaps, surrendering to fantasies of omnipotence, to be
the nation-making American plenipotentiary, at work
behind the scenes and playing confidently even with Bolshevik fire.

And what problems were solved? Nasser solved no
problems. Mr. Kedourie doubts that he needed "to call
on the resources of American political science for such
lessons in tyranny. What does remain most puzzling,"
he says, "is why it was thought that the imparting of such
lessons could advance the interests of the United States,

or even contribute to the welfare of the Egyptian people."

For an American, the most intriguing question is this: Whence the passion for social theory among these high functionaries of the advertising world? How did executive types ever learn of such things?

READING *The Sound and the Fury* last night, I came upon words in Quentin Compson's thought that belonged to E. E. Cummings and the thirties, not to the year 1910. "Land of the kike home of the wop," says Compson to himself when he buys a bun from a small Italian girl. This I would have read without flinching in Chicago but in Jerusalem I flinched and put the book down. Returning to it next day, I found Faulkner guilty of no offense. It's possible that people at the turn of the century were saying "land of the kike" and that Faulkner didn't borrow it from Cummings. I had been telling Shahar when we were walking in the Gai-Hinnom that I hadn't liked it when David Ben-Gurion on his visits to the United States would call upon American Jews to give up their illusions about goyish democracy and emigrate full speed to Israel. As if America's two-hundred-year record of liberal democracy signified nothing. If Israel were governed as Egypt is, or Syria, would I have come here at all?

But then, to its more severe leftist critics, some of them Jews, Israel is not the "democratic exception" it is said to be. The New Left sees it as a reactionary small country. Its detractors tell you how it abuses its Arab population and, to a lesser extent, Jewish immigrants from North Africa and the Orient. It is occasionally denounced by some Israelis as corrupt, "Levantine," theocratic. Gossip traces the worst of the Israeli financial swindles to the most observant of Orthodox Jews. I am often told that the old Ashkenazi leaders were unimaginative, that the new

Rabin group lacks stature, that Ben-Gurion was a terrible old guy but a true leader, that the younger generation is hostile to North African and Asian Jews. These North African and Oriental immigrants are blamed for bringing a baksheesh mentality to Israel; the intellectuals are blamed for letting the quality of life (a deplorable phrase) deteriorate—I had hoped that six thousand miles from home I would hear no more about the quality of life—and then there is the Palestinian question, the biggest and most persistent of Israel's headaches: "We came here to build a just society. And what happened immediately?"

I speak of this to Shahar. He says to me, "Where there is no paradox there is no life."

IN Jakov Lind's interesting brief book on Israel, Ben-Gurion is quoted as saying, "The Jews know hardly anything of a hell that might await them. Their hell is a personal dissatisfaction with themselves if they are mediocre."* Jews do, it is well known, make inordinate demands upon themselves and upon one another. Upon the world, too. I occasionally wonder whether that is why the world is so uncomfortable with them. At times I suspect that the world would be glad to see the last of its Christianity, and that it is the persistency of the Jews that prevents it. I say this remembering that Jacques Maritain once characterized European anti-Semitism of the twentieth century as an attempt to get rid of the moral burden of Christianity. And what is it that has led the Jews to place themselves, after the greatest disaster of their history, in a danger zone? A Jewish professor at Harvard recently said to me, "Wouldn't it be the most horrible of ironies if the Jews had collected themselves conveniently in one country for a second Holocaust?" This is a thought that sometimes crosses Jewish minds. It is accompanied by the further reflection (partly proud, mostly bitter) that we Jews seem to have a genius for finding the heart of the crisis.

*The Trip to Jerusalem (New York, 1973).

THE Valley of Jehosaphat, with its tombs. A narrow road, and on the slopes acres and acres of stone. Caves, graves, litter, fallen rocks, and in tiny schoolrooms Arab boys singing their lessons. Even in November the place is uncomfortably warm. The Jordanians built a road over Jewish graves. The municipality of Jerusalem is planning to build a new road and will tear the Jordanian one up. The Herodian relics are all that relics should be—columns distorted, well worked over by time, Absalom's tomb with its bulbous roof and odd funnel tapering out of it. The armies of the dead in all directions, interminable. A fine thing to obsess yourself with, burial and lamentation and lying about under the walls of Jerusalem waiting for the Messiah's trumpet to sound. A few Arab hens are scratching up dust and pecking. Not a breakfast egg comes to the table that isn't death-speckled. Parties of American girls come down the slope in their dungarees, with sweaters tied by their sleeves about the waist. Above, to the left, a Muslim cemetery. The great Golden Gate that will open when the Redeemer appears stands sealed. Just beyond, the Garden of Gethsemane. As its name indicates, it was an olive grove. Now pines, cypresses, and eucalyptus trees grow there below the domes of the Russian Orthodox church. Opposite it there are olives still, which Arabs are harvesting with long poles. They hit the branches, they thresh the leaves with their sticks, and the fruit rains down.

As we go up into the Via Dolorosa, we hear an exciting

jingle. Arab boys are racing their donkeys down the hill.
You look for sleighs and frost when you hear this jingle-
belling. Instead, there are boys stern and joyous, gallop-
ing hell-bent on their donkeys toward the Lions' Gate.

"Rode from Ramlah to Lydda," Herman Melville
wrote in his travel journal of 1857. ". . . A mounted es-
cort of some 30 men, all armed. Fine riding. Musket-
shooting. Curvetting & caracoling of the horsemen. Out-
riders. Horsemen riding to one side, scorning the perils."
And a few days later, on the barrenness of Judea, "whit-
ish mildew pervading whole tracts of landscape—bleached
—leprosy—encrustation of curses—old cheese—bones of
rocks,—crunched, gnawed, & mumbled—mere refuse &
rubbish of creation—like that laying outside of Jaffa Gate
—all Judea seems to have been accumulations of this
rubbish. . . . *No moss as in other ruins—no grace of decay
—no ivy—the unleavened nakedness of desolation*—whit-
ish ashes—lime-kilns. . . . *Village of Lepers*—houses facing the wall—Zion. Their park, a dung-heap.—They sit by
the gates asking alms,—then whine—avoidance of them &
horror. . . . *Wandering among the tombs*—till I began to
think myself one of the possessed with devils."

ANWAR Sadat's American visit. You have to discuss this with Israelis before they will consent to talk about anything else. An indignant librarian, a middle-aged woman whose face is so hot it is almost fragrant with indignation, demands of me in a super-distinguished all but Oxonian accent, *"How* do you account for it!"

I shrug. This is what I would say if I did answer her: Americans love to open their hearts to foreign visitors. These visitors are sometimes treated as if they were the heroes of an Arabian Nights' tale. We'll show them how good we all are and well-meaning and generous and open-minded and even-handed. We will be full of emotion and the visitors will be correspondingly full of emotion, and after they have been wined and feted and dined and toasted and televised and paraded and clapped and the supplying of loans and atomic plants and military hardware has been discussed they will love us. I trust that they will give us better love than they are getting from us, for ours is a very low-quality upward-seeping vegetable-sap sort of love, as short-lived as it is spontaneous. As soon as they leave they are forgotten. An old Mormon missionary in Nauvoo once gripped my knee hard as we sat side by side, and he put his arm about me and called me "Brother." We'd only met ten minutes before. He took me to his good bosom. His eyes began to mist. I was a prospect, an exotic prospect in old tennis shoes and a sweatshirt. His heart opened to me. It opened like a cuckoo clock. But it did not give me the time of day.

"But don't Americans know that Sadat was a Nazi?" the librarian says.

Well, yes, well-informed people do have this information in their files. *The New York Times* is sure to have it, but the *Times* as I see it is a government within a government. It has a state department of its own, and its high councils have probably decided that it would be impolitic at this moment to call attention to Sadat's admiration for Hitler.

I tell the lady that I have sent a copy of a eulogy of Hitler written by Sadat in 1953 to Sydney Gruson of the *Times* and also to Katharine Graham of *The Washington Post*.

"Will they print it?" she asked.

"Difficult to guess," I tell her. "The *Times* ought to be stronger in politics than it is in literature, but who knows. Of course it must do financial news and sports well enough. If it covered ball games as badly as it reviews books, the fans would storm it like the Bastille. Book readers evidently haven't got the passionate intensity of sports fans."

What disturbs is whether Americans understand the world at all, whether they are a match for the Russians—the Sadats are in themselves comparatively unimportant. To dissident Russian writers like Lev Navrozov, the Americans can never be a match for the Russians. He quotes from Dostoevski's *The House of the Dead* a conversation between the writer and a brutal murderer, one of those criminals who fascinated him.* I haven't the book handy, so I paraphrase. "Why are you so kind to me?" Dostoevski asks. And the murderer, speaking to one of the geniuses of the nineteenth century, answers, "Because you are so simple that one cannot help feeling sorry for you." Even when he robbed Dostoevski, he pitied him as one might "a little cherub-like child." Navrozov, exceedingly intelligent but, to a Westerner, curiously deformed (how could an independent intellec-

The Education of Lev Navrozov (New York, 1975).

tual in the Soviet Union escape deformity?), sees us, the Americans, as children at whom the Stalins smile through their mustachios. Perhaps there is a certain Vautrin-admiring romanticism in this. Dostoevski, no mean judge of such matters, thought there was much to be said for the murderer's point of view. Navrozov extends the position. Liberal democracy is as brief as a bubble. Now and then history treats us to an interval of freedom and civilization and we make much of it. We forget, he seems to think, that as a species we are generally close to the "state of nature," as Thomas Hobbes described it—a nasty, brutish, pitiless condition in which men are too fearful of death to give much thought to freedom. If Hobbes is too nifty an authority, let us think of the social views of Jimmy Hoffa. Or of the Godfather. Or of Lenin, as Navrozov accurately characterizes him. And this is what America, bubbling with political illusions, is up against. So, at least, Navrozov thinks. Perhaps Alexander Solzhenitsyn agrees with him in part. Apparently Russians are all inclined to see us in this way. My own cousin, Nota Gordon, two years out of the Soviet Union, says to me, "You are no match for them. You do not understand with whom you are dealing."

Nota held the rank of captain in the Russian army and fought the Germans until 1945. He was three times seriously wounded. He has the family look—the brown eyes, arched brows, dark coloring, and white hair. He has, besides, the gold crowns of Russian dental art. Criminals released from prison during the war served in his company. Nota has no swagger but he is war-hardened. There was no food sent to the front lines. You ate frozen potatoes, you foraged, and you stole. You could depend on your criminal soldiers to bring in provisions. "I myself had absolute authority to kill anyone in my command. At my discretion. No explanations necessary," says Nota. We are first cousins but he is Russian, I am an American, and in his Russian eyes an American is amiable, good-natured, attractive perhaps, but undeveloped, helpless: all that Dostoevski was to his fellow convict the murderer.

Nevertheless, I see that in a book called *Things to Come* two Americans who think themselves anything but undeveloped and helpless, Herman Kahn and B. Bruce-Briggs, are not impressed by Russian achievements. "Most striking is the disappointing performance of Soviet foreign and domestic policy since the late 1950s," they wrote in 1972. "In the foreign policy field the Soviets have had an almost uninterrupted series of defeats and disappointments. They have failed to extend their influence in Europe. . . . Their attempts to ingratiate themselves with India and other neutralist nations have gained them little. . . . For fifteen years the Soviet Union has been supporting the Arabs against Israel in the Middle East and all they have to show for it is the humiliation of their protégés and the capture and destruction of their equipment by Israel. The Arabs have shown no inclination toward Communist ideology and their oil continues to flow to the West. (The only other choice for the Arabs is to leave their oil in the ground.)"

I copy this out for my own entertainment—a specimen of illusionless American political analysis. These views—no substitute for common sense—are based upon careful staff work at the Hudson Institute. The Messrs. Kahn and Bruce-Briggs say in a prefatory note that their book is "basically an organizational product. All of the staff at Hudson have contributed in some way to this work, as have the thousands of people with whom we have discussed these issues at meetings, seminars, and briefings at the Institute and other locations around the world."

WHAT the literary imagination faces in these
political times. One of the finest Israeli writers,
A. B. Yehoshua, speaks about this in an excellent book of interviews, *Unease in Zion,* edited by Ehud
ben Ezer. "It is true," Yehoshua writes, "that because
our spiritual life today cannot revolve around anything
but these questions [political questions], when you en-
gage in them without end you cannot spare yourself,
spiritually, for other things. Nor can you attain the true
solitude that is a condition and prerequisite of creation,
the source and its strength. Rather, you are continuously
summoned to solidarity, summoned from within yourself
rather than by any external compulsion, because you live
from one newscast to the next, and it becomes a solidarity
that is technical, automatic from the standpoint of its
emotional reaction, because by now you are completely
built to react that way and to live in tension. Your emotional reactions to any piece of news about an Israeli
casualty, a plane shot down, are pre-determined. . . .
Hence the lack of solitude, the inability to be alone in the
spiritual sense, and to arrive at a life of intellectual creativity." During the Six Day War, Yehoshua says that he
felt himself linked to a great event, that he was within a
historic wave and at one with its flow. This was a pleasant
and elevating feeling. But today, unable to see the end
of war, he has lost the sensation of being borne upon any
such wave. "You do not achieve peace from history," he
says. "The feeling of being swept along and of uncertainty as regards the future prevents you from seeing

things in any perspective whatsoever. . . . You live the moment, without any perspective, but you cannot break free of the moment, forget the moment. You cannot cut yourself off and not read newspapers or stop hearing the news over the radio for weeks on end, as you could six or seven years ago."

It is slightly different with us. Our media make crisis chatter out of news and fill our minds with anxious phantoms of the real thing—a summit in Helsinki, a treaty in Egypt, a constitutional crisis in India, a vote in the U.N., the financial collapse of New York. We can't avoid being politicized (to use a word as murky as the condition it describes) because it is necessary after all to know what is going on. Worse yet, what is going on will not let us alone. Neither the facts nor the deformations, the insidious platitudes of the media (tormenting because the underlying realities are so huge and so terrible), can be screened out. The study of literature is itself heavily "politicized." There is a clever, persistent young woman who writes to me from Italy, who insists upon giving the most ordinary occurrences in my novels a political interpretation. A cafeteria lunch in New York actually refers to a meeting in Canada between Churchill and Roosevelt, and a tussle with a drunk in the hallway of a rooming house corresponds to D-Day. Everything reflects the significant event, for the significant event is beyond question historical and political, not private. She thinks that it is sly of me to deny this.

Not to submit to what societies and governments consider to be important. Stendhal's heroes, when they are in prison, choose to think above love. E. E. Cummings, locked up by the French government, finds his aesthetic paradise in the detention camp of Ferté Macé. The bravest of modern writers are the Mandelstams and the Sinyavskys. Before he died of cold, hunger, and exhaustion in Siberia, Osip Mandelstam recited his poems to other convicts, at their request. Andrei Sinyavsky, in his prison journal, concentrates on art. Perhaps to remain a

poet in such circumstances is also to reach the heart of
politics. Then human feelings, human experience, the
human form and face, recover their proper place—the
foreground.

MY friend John Auerbach comes up from Caesarea to see me. A kibbutznik seaman, he has just returned from a voyage. I have known him for only a few years but he has become a dear friend. I had been warned that as I grew older the difficulty of forming new friendships would be great. On the contrary, I find it much easier now at sixty to draw near to people. John looks too much the writer—slight in person, delicate —to be a chief engineer. He does, however, hold an engineer's ticket and can do complicated emergency repairs in mid-ocean. Boyish, bearded (the beard is short and copper-brown), nervous, a bit high, thinner than when I saw him last, he carries a cardboard valise containing books and booze and pajamas and a house present. He is delighted to be here, and he is suffering—the one activates the other. He is grieving for his son. Adam Auerbach served in an electronic-warfare unit and was returning from a military action when the helicopter in which he was flying crashed. We embrace and then we go out-of-doors with a bottle to have a drink and get some sun. Even on a sunny morning the stone buildings of Jerusalem chill your hands and feet. Stepping out, I feel a bit numb, like a wasp in autumn. We sit on a stone wall over the garden and drink aquavit. He wants to talk. He loves books passionately, he wants to discuss American literature, to hear marvelous things from me. But I can see that the big current of his suffering has begun to run heavily. *He* has returned from a voyage, *he* is out in the sun shining from the hills of Moab, *he* is drinking aquavit with a dear friend, looking over at Mount Zion. But his son is *dead*.

At sixteen John escaped from the Warsaw ghetto, leaving behind his parents and his sister. They were killed. Everyone was killed. John somehow obtained Polish seaman's papers, and for several years he worked in the engine rooms of German freighters. When the war ended he came to Israel via Cyprus, joined Kibbutz Sdot Yam, married, and had two children. His first wife died of cancer about ten years ago and he has married again. He says, "I ask myself in what ways my life has not been typical. For a Jew from Eastern Europe it has been completely typical—war, death of mother, death of father, death of sister, four years in disguise among Germans, death of wife, death of son. Thirty years of hard work, planting and harvesting in the kibbutz. Nothing exceptional."

John sails infrequently now. He doesn't like the new huge tankers. Supermechanized, ultraefficient, they give the crew no time in foreign ports. The cargo on the voyage from which he has just returned was Dead Sea potash. They were to bring home Italian steel. North of Naples they had bad weather and engine trouble, but they reached their harbor and anchored near two Japanese ships. On the pilot's advice they were moved farther into port by two tugs. Within five hours John had repaired the engines, but the port officials claimed that the ship was incapacitated and demanded that the captain post a twenty-thousand-dollar bond against expenses that might be run up by his "crippled ship." True, the ship had had to be moved into its berth by the tugs but it had been crippled only briefly. Well, this matter was in dispute. The ship lay unloaded and demurrage fees mounted—in brief, a holdup by local racketeers. The same everywhere, now. Everybody has some con going, says John, who loves American slang. The home office in Haifa was trying to get protection from the insurance company. There were long days in port with nothing to do. The town was covered in potash dust. Waiters and bartenders wiped dishes

and glasses continually. Brushing at dust was the com-
monest gesture in town. A community of about twenty
thousand people had traffic jams worthy of Rome, cars
as a matter of course rushing into the reserved bus lanes,
screwing everything up and honking madly. It all came
to a panting standstill morning and evening without fail.
To get away from the traffic snarl you could climb a
nearby mountain and come down to a deserted beach,
similar to the beach at Sdot Yam. John and his dog,
Mississippi, went there every day. The German tourists
had gone home, the bathing cabins were nailed shut. It
was lovely, the small waves coming in steadily. In little
pangs, said John.

Part of the American Sixth Fleet was anchored nearby.
The aircraft carrier *John F. Kennedy,* with its helicopters,
reminded John of the death of his son. He passed the time
with young American sailors. On shore leave they wear
civilian clothing now. This probably makes them less
rowdy. One of the boys was from Oklahoma, near Tulsa.
He had heard of Israel, but only just, and he was not especially interested. John was delighted by this. A clean
young soul, he said. Such ignorance was refreshing. The
young sailor knew nothing about holocausts or tanks in
the desert or terrorist bombs.

Back at sea, John had to stand double watches in the
engine room because he was shorthanded. Off duty, he
read in his cabin and chatted with his confidante, Mississippi. The crew said he was drinking himself silly in his
quarters. When the ship passed Stromboli at night, there
was a streak of crimson lava flowing from the volcano
and the sailors wouldn't leave the television set to look at
this natural phenomenon. But an owl from the island,
disturbed by the sparks, flew out to the ship and was dis-
covered next day on the mast. One of the young sailors
carried it down. Then an engine man from the Balkans
said, "In our village we nailed owls to the church door
when we caught them." They shut the owl in the paint
locker while they debated what to do with it, and in the
night John set it free. The bird scratched his arm rather

badly. "Go back to Stromboli, you dumb bastard," he said. So it flew off and the ship continued on its foul way. It's the water pumped into the tanks for ballast and then pumped out again that pollutes the seas, says John.

BEFORE I left Chicago, the art critic Harold Rosenberg said to me, "Going to Jerusalem? And wondering whether people will talk freely? You've got to be kidding, they'll talk your head off." He spoke as a Jew to a Jew about Jewish powers of speech. In flight, if the door of your plane comes open you are sucked into space. Here in Jerusalem, when you shut your apartment door behind you you fall into a gale of conversation—exposition, argument, harangue, analysis, theory, expostulation, threat, and prophecy. From diplomats you hear cagey explanations; from responsible persons, cautious and grudging statements rephrasing and amending your own questions; from parents and children, deadly divisions; from friends who let themselves go, passionate speeches, raging denunciation of Western Europe, of Russia, of America. I listen carefully, closely, more closely than I've ever listened in my life, utterly attentive, but I often feel that I have dropped into a shoreless sea.

The subject of all this talk is, ultimately, survival—the survival of the decent society created in Israel within a few decades. At first this is hard to grasp because the setting is so civilized. You are in a city like many another—well, not quite, for Jerusalem is the only ancient city I've ever seen whose antiquities are not on display as relics but are in daily use. Still, the city is a modern city with modern utilities. You shop in supermarkets, you say good morning to friends on the telephone, you hear symphony orchestras on the radio. But suddenly the music stops and a terrorist bomb is reported. A new explosion outside a

34

coffee shop on the Jaffa Road: six young people killed and thirty-eight more wounded. Pained, you put down your civilized drink. Uneasy, you go out to your civilized dinner. Bombs are exploding everywhere. Dynamite has just been thrown in London; the difference is that when a bomb goes off in a West End restaurant the fundamental right of England to exist is not in dispute.

Yet here you sit at dinner with charming people in a dining room like any other. You know that your hostess has lost a son; that her sister lost children in the 1973 war; that in this Jerusalem street, coolly sweet with night flowers and dark green under the lamps, many other families have lost children. And on the Jaffa Road, because of another bomb, six adolescents—two on a break from night school—stopping at a coffee shop to eat buns, have just died. But in the domestic ceremony of passed dishes and filled glasses thoughts of a destructive enemy are hard to grasp. What you do know is that there is one fact of Jewish life unchanged by the creation of a Jewish state: you cannot take your right to live for granted. Others can; you cannot. This is not to say that everyone else is living pleasantly and well under a decent regime. No, it means only that the Jews, because they are Jews, have never been able to take the right to live as a natural right.

To be sure, many Israelis refuse to admit that this historic uneasiness has not been eliminated. They seem to think of themselves as a fixed power, immovable. Their point has been made. They are a nation among nations and will always remain so. You must tear your mind away from this conviction, as you must tear it from "civilized" appearances, in order to reach reality. The search for relief from the uneasiness is what is real in Israel. Nationalism has no comparable reality. To say, as George Steiner says, that Zionism was created by Jewish nationalists who drew their inspiration from Bismarck and followed a Prussian model can't be right. The Jews did not become nationalistic because they drew strength from their worship of anything resembling Germanic *Blut und Eisen* but because they alone, amongst the peoples of the earth, had not established a natural right to exist unquestioned in the lands of their birth. This right is still clearly not granted them, not even in the liberal West.

At the same time Jews are called upon (by Mr. Steiner in *The Listener**) and call upon themselves to be more just and more moral than others.

*"Israel's Failure of Vision," *The Listener*, September 18, 1975.

MR. D of the Foreign Ministry is wearing a suit. Israelis seldom dress up. Even more exceptional is Mr. D's necktie, for in Israel gentlemen favor the Whitmanesque—or Ben-Gurionesque—open collar. I have been told that Winston Churchill gravely disapproved of Ben-Gurion's informality of dress, but I cannot vouch for this. Mr. D, however, is a proper diplomat who grew up under the British Mandate. Although he fought against it, he loves England and is happier in London or Oxford than anywhere else in the world except Israel. He gives me a brief rundown of the diplomatic posts he has held. He doesn't actually say that he hates Sweden—I say it for him. He intimates that in Stockholm everyone was very correct, faultless, but perhaps also heartless. France? Well, what can one do about the French, they are so wonderful, they are so disagreeable. France is an open society for those who are willing to become French. Americans? A strange and mixed lot. Decent people but crude and lacking finish—not to be compared with the best products of English culture. We are drinking tea, English tea with milk in it. On every archway of my flat there is a mezuzah. Through the lattice windows we see Mount Zion and the Muslim parapets. Late afternoon light on the stones only increases their stoniness. Yellow and gray, they have achieved their final color; the sun can do no more with them.

I try Mr. D with one of my questions. He has worked in Washington. Do Americans know what is going on in the world? Admittedly, he replies, the Americans are well informed, their information-gathering apparatus is formidable. But to be well informed, I persist, is not the same as understanding what goes on. My correct visitor grants me this. Does he agree with the Armenian Archbishop and with M. Tatu of *Le Monde* that Kissinger has outwitted the Russians by getting Egypt to accept the Sinai agreement? Mr. D does not think that Mr. Kissinger has foiled Russia in the Middle East. The inevitable speculation follows: What *is* Kissinger? The Israelis are profoundly and bitterly intrigued by him. How *did* he get his power, anyway? We go over the usual points. Without a real base, he has the wizard exotic aura of the clever Jew, the *Jud Süss,* the financial manager or business agent of small German princedoms. He has a bold hand, he is cagey, he is a jet-setter, a glamour-lover, and a publicity expert. He seems to understand that since television has created an entertainment culture in the United States, you must join the entertainment world if you have no other power base, becoming something of a star. Kissinger has done this brilliantly. Perhaps it is after all his dramatic talent that accounts for everything. His good friend Danny Kaye can be serious as well as comic, and Kissinger can be playful. In diplomacy he is too roughly playful. Israel's present ambassador has been dominated by the overmastering Kissinger. I have been told that he got Simchah Dinitz to lobby for a Sinai agreement. It was infra dig for an ambassador to haunt the corridors of the Senate Office Building, to solicit votes in congressional offices, said my informants. Israel is poorly represented in Washington. For Israel, the Washington job is the most important of all diplomatic assignments and yet inadequate people are continually sent over. But then Israel is poorly governed now. The founding generation has no adequate successors.

Does Mr. D think that the Russians, disappointed in their efforts in the Arab world, might like to resume diplomatic relations with Israel? That is up to the Russians, says Mr. D. "If we approach them they will take it for a sign of weakness. They will come to us if and when it seems profitable to them to re-establish such relations. To open their embassy in Ramat-Gan would bring them certain advantages. They could more easily gather information. As it is, they must depend upon their agents. Possibly they will get the Poles to come back and do the job for them."

Mr. Kissinger, in Geneva, arranged private talks between Andrei Gromyko and the Israelis. This was in December 1973. Gromyko, though he seems publicly surly, sour, rude and inflexible, knows how to reverse himself. The forbidding Gromyko addressed Foreign Minister Abba Eban with sweetness, as an old colleague should. How many wonderful occasions they had shared. They had quarreled, yes, and their disputes had at times been murderous, but on the human level—and Gromyko is after all human—there are private sentimental attachments.

I have been told often by people who should know (again a few days ago by a young American woman who had just received her Ph.D. in Russian literature) that Russian, the language itself, is one of the strongholds of the human heart. It has what social scientists would call "charismatic depths." A commonplace Russian conversation will contain most affectionate expressions. And even if you condemn people to death you are obliged by the genius of the language to frame the death sentence in loving words. There would seem to be a struggle between light and darkness within the mother tongue, and perhaps Russian history is in part a rebellion against these loving expressions by which "realistic" people feel themselves betrayed. They speak loving words and they may feel that a mind stirred by love is dangerous. Peril mobilizes your defenses, and then you murder because your soul has been moved. But a Gromyko can feel secure enough behind the mountain range of corpses to speak sweetly in private to the representative of a tiny country with whom he is having an intimate cup of tea. He told Eban that Russia has never been Israel's enemy. Israel was born with the blessings of the Soviet Union.

That is true enough. But what of the billions in Russian
military aid to Syria, and what of the SAM missiles, the
arming of Palestinian terrorists, the denunciations in the
Soviet press and in the U.N.? Ah well, it is true we are
against the territorial expansion of Israel, and we cannot
accept aggression, occupation, and the rest of it. But we
are not really unfriendly toward Israel. From first to last
our attitude has been consistent.

Hearing of such a conversation, you get the feeling
that Israel is something like an insecure tooth on which
the Russians don't choose to use the pincers. They will
work it back and forth and when it is sufficiently loose
they will take it out with their fingers.

The intelligent Mr. D is well-bred and speaks de-
cently, exaggerates nothing, and is devoid of pretensions.
What Mr. D says, and he says it quietly, is that for him
it is bliss to be in England.

Last week, the novelist Amos Oz observed to me that
Israel contains more different visions of Heaven than
any outsider can imagine. Everyone who came over
brought his own dream of Paradise with him. On Oz's
own kibbutz, people work hard until 2 p.m. Then they
wash and rest and dress, and after lunch, many of them
being Russian in origin, they read serious books and
listen to music; they spend their afternoons and evenings
gravely discussing Marxism. Their greatest pleasure is to
talk in the old way about revolution and socialism and
the future of mankind. The German Jews here often rest
in a *Kultur* paradise, reading Homer and Plato and
Goethe, and listening to Mozart.

THE old barber at the King David Hotel, Ephraim Mizrahi, a native of Jerusalem, asks me how old I am. He then says, "I, too, am sixty." We are speaking Spanish—Ladino, rather. He is a charmer: his hands shake a bit but he gives an excellent haircut. His blue eyes are small and overhung with wild white hairs. I speak to him about Hubert H. Humphrey, and a blue flame awakens again in those two embers. A sort of senile strength and cheer straighten his body. He adores Hubert H. Humphrey. Signed photos of Humphrey hang on every wall. He has often cut Humphrey's hair. He has received senatorial and Vice-Presidential letters from Humphrey. I take the trouble to go around and read them. They are rich in congressional corn. Everything is big and open, congratulatory, wonderful and frank. "How do you like that?" says Ephraim. "*¡Un hombre tan importante que me escribe and me ha dado su re-trato—a mí, un barbero sencillo!*" The senator looks extremely healthy and so does his wife. They are holding hands and strolling, dressed in sportswear, through the flowers.

Feeble Mizrahi returns to his snipping. I wonder whether my ears will be safe when he unfolds his straight razor. But that is merely peripheral. What goes through my mind is that Humphrey is really an awfully clever politician. Thousands of influential American Jews, big givers, stop at the King David. How ingenious of Humphrey to win the barber's heart and cover the walls of his shop with letters and photographs. And perhaps

41

Humphrey really lost his heart to the old boy. Anyway, no harm has been done to Mizrahi, sighing and doddering and clipping behind me. Humphrey is, indeed, a friend of Israel and could be counted on to be one even if he had become President. Alexandra and I saw Humphrey not long ago at a banquet given in the White House for Harold Wilson. Wilson, fatty, stooped, and short, without the slightest interest in the people being introduced to him, his longish white hair lying on the dusty collar of his dinner jacket, was merely getting through the evening, longing for his bed and his mystery novel. And there was Humphrey, slender, fit, elastic, eager, rosy, and garrulous. Alexandra and I had just come up from the lobby. On the ground floor, a young Marine in dress uniform, covered with campaign ribbons, was playing baroque Italian music on a harp. We checked our coats, another uniformed Marine escorted Alexandra up the stairs, and there was a Marine orchestra playing tunes from Broadway musicals. Then we entered the East Room and joined the other guests. I knew, or thought I knew, many of them, having seen their faces on television and in the papers. But this was illusory. I have never met Cary Grant or Danny Kaye—I only feel that I have. Senator Humphrey was the only man there with whom I could claim to be acquainted. "There's someone I know," I said to Alexandra, and I introduced her to the senator, who shook our hands. But he was in one of his public states. The fit was on him. He couldn't bear to be confined to the two of us. He was looking for someone more suitable, for the most suitable encounter, the one it could be death to miss. He was gripped by an all but demonic desire for the optimum encounter. He touched our hands, he looked beyond us and was gone. Nelson Rockefeller suffered from the same disorder. It was only the old senators without Presidential ambitions who did not hasten from guest to guest. Wrinkled senior elephants like Hugh Scott waited patiently for their food.

Alexandra smiled at me and said, "Senator Humphrey

doesn't remember you." But he was next to her at table and she told me after dinner that he had suddenly remembered me. "Minneapolis, and so on." She rather liked him.

Kissinger was deep in conversation with Danny Kaye. Their arms about each other. One of Kissinger's assistants earnestly said, "That is an old relationship and a very meaningful one." Nelson Rockefeller, stockier and shorter than I had thought him to be, crossed the room to shake my hand. He had taken me for someone else and recognized his error in mid-course when it was too late to turn aside. We did the handshake bit, I murmured my meaningless name, and the Vice President went on to seek a more significant encounter. This gave me some sense of what it was to be had in thrall, like the poor knight in Keats's "La Belle Dame sans Merci"—only in public life.

When we left, the attendants below could not get us a cab. They said, "Cabs won't come to the White House."

"Why?"

"Well, they're sore at us. They answer a call and by the time they get here the party's taken a ride with somebody else. So now they say to hell with the White House."

We were advised to go on foot, along the old State Department Building and out through the gate to Pennsylvania Avenue. And so we did, under a cold rain that ruined Alexandra's silk shoes. There was little traffic on Pennsylvania Avenue. I planted myself in mid-street and stopped a cab. The driver refused to take us to our hotel. He was Virginia-bound, he said, and he drove off. Then the police pulled up and said, "What are you doing here?" They took in Alexandra's evening dress and were astonished at us. The place was dangerous. From the curb they kept an eye on the situation. They didn't want the President's guests mugged after a bash. The White House behind us was filled with light. Guests were still dancing in the beautiful old rooms.

By and by an old black man pulled up in his cab and

took us out of the chill rain. "Awright," he said, "get in."
And we went home.

We had eaten turtle soup and dark-gray slices of squab
and wild rice and palm-heart salad and a chocolate something for dessert, and we had drunk California wines.
We had shaken hands with Danny Kaye and with the
President and the First Lady and Kirk Douglas and Senator William Fulbright and Beverly Sills and Margaret
Truman Daniels and Harold Wilson and Nelson Rockefeller (a matter of mistaken identity) and with Hubert
Humphrey and with many wives—wives who might have
belonged to an organization called Prom Queens of the
Thirties. I got into bed at the Enfant Plaza Hotel and I
understood a little the phenomenon described by neurol-
ogists as an insult to the brain. As I closed my eyes, the
night opened mercifully before me and my spirit grate-
fully left this world.

THE journal of Andrei Sinyavsky, whose pseudonym is Abram Tertz, has not yet been published in English. I have the French edition. I translate: ". . . no longer men but great sweeps. Spaces, fields, not characters," he says, speaking of his fellow prisoners. "Human frontiers blur where they touch the infinite. Beyond biography. Man, each man, eludes biography. When you try to support your weight on 'personal characteristics' you sink up to the waist. Personality is a ditch covered lightly by a growth of psychological traits, temperaments, habits, ways of doing things. I have no sooner taken a step toward an approaching stranger than I find that I have fallen into a hole." And, "We have come into the world in order to understand certain things. Only a few things, very few, but exceedingly important. . . . Art is a meeting place. Of the author and the object of his love, of spirit and matter, of truth and fantasy, of the line traced by a pencil, the contour of a body, of one word with another. These meetings are rare, unexpected, 'Is that you?' 'Is it you?' Recognizing each other, both parties are seized by a frenzy, and clasp hands. In these gestures of surprise and joy we see art."

The exhaustive report of Amnesty International, an unofficial group concerned with prisoners' rights, has been released in London to Reuters, UPI, AP. It deals with prisoners of conscience and political dissidents in Russia who suffer so desperately in the camps that they inflict fantastic injuries on themselves. "Hunger, excessive work, and other privations, including medical

45

neglect, have led some prisoners to commit suicide." They feign escape in order to be shot by their guards. They practice "collective self-mutilation." Evidence has been taken from Edward Kuznetov, among others: "I have seen convicts swallow huge numbers of nails and quantities of barbed wire. I have seen them swallow mercury thermometers . . . chess pieces, dominoes, needles, ground glass, spoons, knives, and many other similar objects. I have seen convicts sew up their mouths and eyes with thread or wire, sew buttons to their bodies or nail their testicles to a bed, swallow a nail bent like a hook and then attach this hook by way of a thread so that the door cannot be opened without pulling the 'fish' inside out. I have seen convicts cut open the skin on their arms and legs and peel it off as if it were a stocking or cut out lumps of flesh from their stomachs or their legs, roast them and eat them, or let blood drip from a slit vein into a tureen." But enough!

The report states, "There are at least 10,000 political and religious prisoners in the U.S.S.R. today." Held under conditions that "violate international standards for the treatment of prisoners."

How much of this is known in the free countries of the West? The information is to be found in the daily papers. We are informed about everything. We know nothing.

GUNS are a common sight in Jerusalem at any time. In every quarter of the city, as in every community in Israel, there are armed civilian patrols that include students. Daily, before schools open in the morning, they are examined by parents for bombs. Arab students were asked to participate on the campus of the Hebrew University but refused. In my opinion it was a mistake to ask that they be part of such patrols. They are trying to avoid a charge of "collaboration." The status of the Israeli Arabs is ambiguous anyway. They do and do not enjoy equal rights. They cause great uneasiness. More than once I have been told that the Palestine Liberation Organization would like to provoke riots in the Old City and the authorities fear that explosions like the one the other night in which six adolescents were killed may provoke them. These would be politically disastrous, since the Arabs have demonstrated their control of the U.N. General Assembly and could easily put through punitive resolutions. The PLO is said to have circulated in the U.N. photographs of the youthful victims with the claim that they have been "executed." Fatah terrorists in the Golan recently shot three young men. They came over the Syrian border with guns and hatchets, intending to cut off the heads of their victims—this according to the deposition of the terrorist captured earlier. Terrorist violence always threatens and often occurs. One has to learn to live with the rumors. I heard the other day that another bomb had been found and dismantled in Jerusalem. My friend Joseph Ben-David, professor of sociology at the Hebrew University, assured me that there had been no bomb, but that same day the dismantling of a new bomb was reported in the papers. And, toward midnight, party guests excuse themselves to go on patrol duty.

We are having tea and cake with Shula and David Shahar and the poet Dennis Silk, and I report a conversation I had with Mahmud Abu Zuluf, the editor of *El Kuds,* the largest Arab newspaper in Jerusalem. The moderate Abu Zuluf is hated by the leftists. His life and the lives of his children have been threatened. His automobile was once blown up, but he continues to follow the line of conciliation and peace. His office is furnished like the waiting room of a parking lot—seats covered in dark plastic, a desk on which people sit as well as write, a pleasant relaxed dustiness here, a place where no one fusses over trifles. There is one work of art in the office, facing the editor: the picture of a pretty kitty with huge eyes, a creature too young to look so amorous. The editor is stout and large—a very large, unmenacing, and even dreamy round-faced man, wearing what the English call a lounging suit. He has on gaudy socks, and his feet are enormous. He doesn't so much shake your hand as gather it into his own. I'm prepared for a most pleasant snow job. Who am I that he should tell me what he actually thinks? He presses a button—like any person who is anyone in Jerusalem, he can ring for an attendant. Coffee is ordered.

It is David Farhi who has brought me to *El Kuds.* Farhi, an Arabist, held the post of Adviser on Arab Affairs to the West Bank Command and is a friend of Mayor Kollek's. Quickly drinking down his coffee, he excuses himself; he wants me to have an uninhibited chat with Abu Zuluf. So the editor and I sip supersweet stuff from the tiny cups, and while composing machines clatter in the rooms beyond he tells me—his mood is somewhere between boredom and passion—that the Jews must give ground in East Jerusalem, they must divide authority with the Arabs. They are too reluctant to accept realities, too slow. The longer they wait the worse things will be. The Arabs are continually gaining strength while Israel becomes weaker. Between cloudiness and intensity, sometimes vague, sometimes opinionated, Abu Zuluf taps hard on the desk top with the flat of his hand and says, "More war, more men lost, more dependency upon your country. While the Arab nations become richer, more modern, more influential. No, Israel must come forward quickly with peace plans and initiate negotiations, show a willingness to negotiate." There are no peaceful moments in Jerusalem, not for those who are making inquiries. You lean back with a cup of coffee to luxuriate in the Oriental conversation of an intelligent man. Immediately you are involved in a tormenting discussion.

Now at tea I tell the Shahars what Abu Zuluf said. I do not like to speak lightly about these matters to them, knowing what they have personally suffered. There are few families in Israel that have not lost sons in the wars. One does not make casual political conversation here. In the next room at this moment, the Shahars' sixteen-year-old son is doing his homework. When he finishes with physics he will practice his Schumann on the piano. Soon he will be old enough for military service. And William Colby of the CIA testified before a congressional committee that in the next war victory might cost Israel nine thousand dead and thirty-six thousand wounded men. Such a victory would signify defeat. The hospitals are still busy with the casualties of the last war. The seventh victim of the Jaffa Road blast, a girl of fifteen, has just died. And U.N. Secretary-General Kurt Waldheim has come to Jerusalem to discuss the Syrian-border question. Mr. Waldheim is not widely admired in Israel. People say that he simply doesn't seem to know what he is talking about. And I am as tactful as possible describing my talk with Abu Zuluf. The Shahars are being polite to me and say little at first. Dennis Silk lowers his eyes. He is one of those bulky men clad in sensitivity. Like me, he's going bald. His hair grows in long and random tufts.

His nose is nobly hooked, and slender. He senses the coming storm and he is flushing.

When Shahar begins his reply, he is at first mild. He does not agree with Abu Zuluf, he says. The Jews have not been inflexible and negative. Concessions are continually offered. They are rejected. The original U.N. partition plan of 1947 was turned down because the Arabs could not tolerate any Jewish state, not even a minuscule one. If a state was what they wanted, they might have had it years ago. They rejected it. And they invaded the country from all sides, hoping to drive the Jews out and take the wealth they had created. This country had been a desert, a land of wandering populations and small stony farms and villages. The Zionists under the Mandate made such economic progress that they attracted Arabs from other areas. This was why the Arab population grew so large. In Jerusalem, Jews had outnumbered Arabs and Christians for a very long time. Before they were driven out of the Old City in the late forties they were a majority. But this was how the world settled Middle Eastern business: Jordan, or Trans-Jordan, was arbitrarily created by the British—yes, by Winston Churchill himself, probably with a pencil, between drinks. "Here, we will give this stuff to those Hashemites." So now you had a "legitimate" nation there. The Egyptians had the slenderest of claims on Sinai during the forties. I know that some of what Shahar is saying is not true, but I say nothing. After World War I, when Britain wanted Sinai part of the Palestine Mandate and France disagreed, it was allotted to Egypt, which had not asked for it. On what was their present claim based, Shahar asks. All these countries, suddenly so proud, nationalistic, and demanding, had been mere bits and pieces of the Ottoman Empire. The Saudis, the dollar-proud defenders of Jerusalem, have little historical connection with the city. "Six generations of my family were born in Jerusalem," says Shahar, growing hot. Shahar is a novelist, and a good one. He loves French literature. Proust he adores. We often chat in French, and a word of that beloved language describes him well. He is *costaud*, sturdy; he has a big frame, broad shoulders, a muscular throat, big veins. The veins are swelling now. I am beginning to irritate him with my American even-handedness, my objectivity at his expense. It is so easy for outsiders to say that there are two sides to the question. What a terrible expression! I am beginning to detest it.

"They don't want our peace proposals. They don't want concessions, they want us destroyed!" Shahar shouts and slams the table. "You don't know them. The West doesn't know them. They will not let us live. We must fight for our lives. It costs the world nothing to discuss, discuss, discuss. And the French are whores and will sell them all the weapons they want, and the British too. And who knows about the Americans! And when the Arabs at last have their way, perhaps the French and the British will be nice and send ships to evacuate our women and children." Now Shahar has named the seldom named dread: he has invoked the nightmare of annihilation. This is what Israel lives with. Although people will not often speak of it, it is always there. I look at Silk's big exquisite face. It is turned downward and he is gazing at the table. As for me I say no more. Can I tell Shahar that the "conscience of the West" will never permit Israel to be destroyed? I can say no such thing. Such grand statements are no longer made; all our hyperbole is nowadays reserved for silence. We know that anything can happen. For the first time in history, the human species as a whole has gone into politics. Everyone is in the act, and there is no telling what may come of it.

A T the Knesset, security measures are very strict. They stop your taxi at the gate and you get out and enter a small office where six or seven soldiers stand about in their berets, machine guns on the floor. They are talking about the movies and Frank Sinatra's coming visit. You state the object of your visit at the desk. You have come to have lunch with Mr. Abba Eban, now a member of the Knesset. Your passport is checked and a phone call is put through to Mr. Eban's office. An old religious Jew in black, bearded, approaches with Talmudic-looking octavo volumes under his insufficient arms. He is cheerful, with good teeth, his nose is rich in capillaries, and he states the object of his visit good-naturedly and at length. Behind him a young couple, demonstrative lovers, stroke each other's heads while waiting for their passes to be issued. The official behind the desk asks to see one of the Talmudic-looking volumes, brings his fingers to his brow, and immerses himself in a dense text. A learned conversation ensues. I wait. Finally I am directed to enter a curtained booth, where a soldier searches me for weapons, feels the lining of my raincoat (the weather is foul today), looks into my hat, has me mount a small platform and feels my legs, pockets, and sides. He opens my fountain pen and examines it. Then he grunts and nods me out of the door toward the great open square before the Parliament Building. The Knesset is grandiose. A country of three and a half million should have something more compact and modest, but the founders are not famous for their good taste. Teddy Kollek has told me that after 1967 Ben-Gurion was all for tearing down the walls of the Old City. "Let it all be open. Make one city, no walls," he argued. "No sense of beauty," says Kollek.

At the information desk the attendants are stern, but the ladies who take your coat gossip amongst themselves. One is knitting a circular object in bright-pink wool. I explain that I have come to lunch, and I am directed down the stairs. There are two dining halls, one for meat-eaters—the ancient dietary segregation. Mr. Eban is waiting. He is reading several newspapers simultaneously—papers under his arms and papers in his fingers. His big eyes further magnified by big tinted lenses seem to flood the small Hebrew print with eye power. His glasses are black-rimmed rectangles, and he bears himself with plump ambassadorial dignity. He and I go to a table in the meat-eaters' hall and order boiled chicken and Wiener schnitzel, respectively. A bottle of Schweppes Bitter Lemon is bumped down on the table and we pour it and sip. Mr. Eban has not yet found what he was looking for in the newspapers and pulls them from under his arms like a man preparing to send semaphore signals. I try to assist him with small talk while he flutters through *Ha'aretz*. At last the meal is served. My perturbed spirit sighs and I pick up a spoon. Mr. Eban is shy but also superconfident—gloomy but not rudely gloomy. He does and does not wish to be where he is. His thoughts go about the world like a satellite. His is a type with which I am completely familiar. The soup plates are removed and the chicken efficiently set before Mr. Eban. It is Jewish chicken, boiled in its skin, sitting upon waves of mashed potatoes and surrounded by shores of rice and brown gravy. My schnitzel is made not of veal but of some other animal tissue, difficult to cut. So I eat my rice and sip the Schweppes. Hungry Mr. Eban is full under the chin. His voice is Oxonian, his views are highly organized. He is not a listener. But I have come to hear what he has to say.

He says that relations between Israel and the United

States have never been better. Israel is receiving more aid from America in this period than in all the years since it was founded. The American role in the war of 1973 has been widely misunderstood. Kissinger did not race off to Moscow out of weakness or because the Russians threatened to intervene. True, he needn't have made it look as though he were answering an imperious summons. Perhaps his speed seemed servile, but what he did was right. America already had the upper hand, and what was necessary at the time was to acknowledge Russia's power in the Middle East and to make the Soviet Union a party to the cease-fire. To push on to Cairo would have meant the loss of another thousand Israelis and might have caused Russia to intervene. What Russia requires is recognition of its great power—deference. It must be invited to sanction all arrangements, it must be consulted. Kissinger had already won his victory.

Then détente is not a meaningless term?

Not at all, if you define it carefully.

And what if it is defined as Solzhenitsyn defined it in his address to the AFL-CIO?

You cannot expect Russian dissidents to describe Russia impartially.

Mr. Eban does not take the severest view possible of the Soviet Union. He does not see it as the worst society in history or as a demonic empire seeking to extend its power, dedicated to the destruction of capitalist democracy. He takes a more balanced view. The Soviet Union may be a wicked superpower but it can be understood, encompassed, and managed. It is not an inhumanly solid and brutal thing. It also blunders, hesitates; its human weaknesses are reassuring. Only see what Mohammed Heikal's book *The Road to Ramadan* reveals about Russia's leaders. Heikal says that on one occasion when he observed them they endlessly circulated a memorandum among half a dozen people before taking a minor decision. Three signatures on a document were needed before an order could be given. What the Russians want is to hold what they already have and to keep the other superpower off-balance. In 1973 they did not urge Syria and Egypt to attack Israel but took a cautious position. They don't want the destruction of Israel—only its withdrawal to the 1967 borders.

The report I had heard of Eban's private conversation with Gromyko was accurate.

As for the PLO, in Eban's view it is an embarrassment to the Russians, and Arafat presents them with many difficulties. The PLO's intervention in Lebanon is not a famous success. The Russians have been disappointed in Egypt. Perhaps they would like Sadat removed. By a *coup d'état*? Mr. Eban is too diplomatic to answer bluntly.

He peels the stippled skin from his drumstick. I smell the steam of boiled fowl, I see the meat, and I attempt the schnitzel again. Institutional food in Israel can be got down if you shut your eyes and think of other things. What comes to mind, unfortunately, is what I saw two days ago in the Old City while strolling with John Auerbach. Young rams were being loaded into a truck for slaughter. They tried to run away. They were grabbed by Arab workmen, picked up by the fleece, and thrown writhing into the truck while everyone shouted curses. "Your sister's cunt," the men were yelling. Off to the side were the malodorous fresh hides of animals just butchered. When will we stop this slaughter and turn to greens and nuts and fruits? It is not a bad question to ask when you hear a highly civilized man discoursing on politics while eating lunch.

Has Mr. Eban ever heard Dr. Kissinger's personal explanation of the policy of détente?

Dr. Kissinger has never sat still long enough to describe this fully to Mr. Eban. People are forever approaching him with messages; Dr. Kissinger is always jumping up.

And now the rain has increased; winter is upon us. Have I transportation? There are no taxis to be had for love or money. With all his newspapers, Eban rises to his feet and offers to drop me off. His car is waiting. We leave the Knesset by the members' exit. Some of the members are full-bearded and wear skull caps. As we drive to the Jaffa Road Eban and I discuss American politicians. It is apparently true that President Gerald Ford only recently learned that the American Embassy was not in the capital of Israel but in Tel Aviv. Eban is reluctant to criticize the President, but he admits that he is no Lyndon Johnson. "*There* was a clever man," says Eban with admiration. I had heard that Johnson once received Eban with the words, "Mr. Ambassador, Ah'm sittin' here scratchin' my ass and thinkin' about Is-ra-el." Eban confirms the truth of this but explains that Johnson spoke in a most friendly manner. Familiarity without contempt. Eban asks me what I think of the Democratic candidates—of Henry Jackson, for instance. Well, I've twice shaken hands with Senator Jackson and I know no more about him than you can learn by shaking a politician's hand. And what of Hubert Humphrey? Senator Humphrey is a better man than most. President Johnson put him in a very bad position. It is a pity that Humphrey was not brave enough to resist. It is true that he is garrulous. Groucho Marx said of him, "I don't know what sort of President he'd make. He talks and talks and talks. He'd make a helluva wife." My theory is that Humphrey learns by talking and that the process is in part educational. A man in public life is far too busy to read much except newspapers and drafts of bills; but Humphrey picks up a good many intelligent opinions, and by debate, repetition, embellishment, and editing he may create something after all. He knows the right thing when he sees it, or when he says it. His record in the Senate is impressive.

The rain has stopped. I get out of Eban's car and thank him and say good-bye. The Jaffa Road, its shops shut since midday for the siesta, is sodden and bleak. I pass the little coffee shop outside which the bomb exploded a few days ago. It is burnt out. A young cabdriver last night told Alexandra and me that he had been about to enter it with one of his friends when another of his pals called to him. "He had something to tell me so I went over to him and just then the bomb went off and my friend was there. So now my friend is dead," said the cabby. His voice, still adolescent, was cracking. "And this is how we live, mister! Okay? We live this way."

EBAN'S attitude toward Russia is shared by many. In a different form, I heard it recently at the Beth Belgia, one of the Hebrew University buildings, from Professor Shlomo Avineri, who is a historian and political scientist. As stated by Professor Avineri, the position is something like this: After World War II, it was widely believed that capitalism had taken a new lease on life. But this was an illusion. The postwar prosperity of capitalism was based on cheap energy and low-priced raw materials from backward countries. The price of these has now risen, and the last free ride of Western capitalism is over—over for all except, perhaps, America. Other Western countries must now prepare to live on a more austere standard. In Eastern Europe, on the other hand, life has immensely improved. The lower classes are beginning to eat well and dress comfortably and live in warm apartments. It is principally the old middle class that is unhappy—the professionals, the intellectuals. And across the face of Europe we will see a gradual evening out of privileges and a redistribution of the good things of life. The Western centers of old Europe are growing dimmer, but Hungary, Bulgaria, Rumania, Poland are brightening up. This, rather than expanding Red imperialism and the subjugation of Europe by Russia, is what we should be considering. If I understand him, Professor Avineri is saying that an independent sort of communism is developing among Russia's satellites and that Western communism is becoming more democratic, less obedient to Moscow. In any case, the world is being transformed, and neither superpower is what so many of us had always assumed it to be.

This is the sort of thing one hears in Paris or Milan rather than Jerusalem. Such a vision of the future evidently grows out of assumptions about the decline of American prestige and influence. It takes for granted that in fighting the extension of communism in Southeast Asia the United States made the greatest mistake in its history. A desire to accept a new view of communism is one of the results of the Vietnam disaster and of America's internal political disorder. Besides, Israel's utter dependency upon the United States leads Israeli intellectuals to hunt for signs of hope in the Communist world. I often wonder why it should rend people's hearts to give up their Marxism. What does it take to extinguish the hopes raised by the October Revolution? How much more do intellectuals need to learn about the U.S.S.R.? Knowing something about life in Communist countries, I disagree completely with Avineri. In my judgment this is a frivolous analysis—heartless, too, if you think how little personal liberty there is in Eastern Europe. One has no business to give away the rights of others. But I look again at Professor Avineri and see that he is an engaging fellow, far from heartless. I conclude that he is only trying out these views. Tomorrow, in another mood, he may take a different line.

D AVID Farhi says that Sadat, on his American visit, proclaimed his Arab loyalties and set himself up as a super-Arab in order to be free from suspicion. The Arab world has accused him of softening. Having made the gestures of solidarity, he is free to detach himself and to deal with internal Egyptian problems —overpopulation, economic stagnation, disease. Professor Michael Brecher, of the Hebrew University, an Israeli of Canadian origin, wonderfully talkative and minutely informed, agrees with Farhi and adds that Sadat's regime is in danger. The Russians are vexed with him. Egyptian university students, a number of whom were junior officers in the war of 1973, are critical and dissatisfied. Egypt's propagandistic revision of the events of the war do not take them in. They know how poorly they were led and how quickly Israel recovered from the defeats of the first days. If the Russians are organizing a *coup d'état*, they have an angry student population trained in warfare to recruit from.

Behind exchanges like this stand images of torpid towns on the Nile and of undernourished people, ill with bilharzia. The world to be coped with is a world in which what has always been has become intolerable. The Egypt of my picture is the Egypt of Edward Lane and other observers and travelers. It extends over the entire region —the Sudan and Ethiopia. It has now been decreed that ages of inertia are at an end, this must be changed, and the change must begin at once. No one can say just what the new imperative will produce. In old age, Tolstoi said to

A. B. Goldenveizer, who often played Chopin for him, "Perhaps it is because I am unwell, but at moments today I am simply driven to despair by everything that is going on in the world: the new form of oath, the revolting proclamation about enlisting university students in the army, the Dreyfus affair, the situation in Serbia, the horrors of the diseases and deaths in the Auerbach quicksilver works. . . . I can't make out how mankind can go on living like this, with the sight of all this horror round them."

Are we wrong to think that our horrors today are much greater? This morning's paper reports that nine men were found dead in an Argentine ditch, blindfolded and shot through the head; that South Moluccans seized a Dutch train and murdered some of the passengers. Scores of people are killed in the streets of Beirut every day; terrorists take hostages in London and explode bombs in Belfast. As an American, I can decide on any given day whether or not I wish to think of these abominations. I need not consider them. I can simply refuse to open the morning paper. In Israel, one has no such choice. There the violent total is added up every day. And nothing can be omitted. The Jerusalemite hooked by world politics cannot forget Gerald Ford and China, Ronald Reagan and California; he is obliged to know that Harold Wilson has just asserted in a speech that England is still a force to be reckoned with. He cannot afford to overlook the latest changes in the strategy of the French Communist Party nor the crises in Portugal and Angola; he must remember the mental character of the Muslim world, the Jews of the Diaspora. Israelis must, in fact, bear in mind four thousand years of Jewish history. The world has been thrown into their arms and they are required to perform an incredible balancing act. Another way of putting it: no people has to work so hard on so many levels as this one. In less than thirty years the Israelis have produced a modern country—doorknobs and hinges, plumbing fixtures, electrical supplies, chamber music, airplanes, teacups. It is both a garrison state and

a cultivated society, both Spartan and Athenian. It tries
to do everything, to understand everything, to make
provision for everything. All resources, all faculties are
strained. Unremitting thought about the world situation
parallels the defense effort. These people are actively,
individually involved in universal history. I don't see how
they can bear it.

A walk in the Old City with Sholem Kahn, who is
on the faculty of the Hebrew University. He
takes me through the Greek section of the Christian quarter and we visit the small Franciscan bookshop.
The old clerk is a Christian Arab who served more than
fifty years ago in the Turkish army and likes to talk about
the barbarous old days. In the windows, Franciscan
translations of medieval Italian travel narratives. "And
how is Father Hoade?" asks Kahn, inquiring about the
translator of these works.

"Oh, he went to Rome and died three years ago."

"Ah, did he. What a pity. Awfully nice fellow," says
Kahn, himself awfully nice. And after all, this is how it
happens. You are born in Ireland, put on a habit, translate medieval Italian travel narratives in Jerusalem, go
to Rome, and die.

Kahn insists on showing me some ancient baths at
the lower end of the Old City and we ask our way through
endless lanes, where kids ride donkeys, kick rubber balls,
scream, fall from wagons, and build small fires in buckets
to warm their fingers, for the weather is cold. A freezing
east wind blows above the arches of the covered streets.
The ancient stone is very cold. The sun does not often get
into these streets. A gang of black Sudanese boys shout
frantic advice at a driver backing his truck into a narrow
lane, scraping the Arabic inscription of a plugged fountain, the gift of some eleventh-century sultan, I imagine.
Kahn asks again for his Turkish baths. A candy seller,
cutting up one of his large flat sticky cakes, a kind of

honeyed millstone, appears indignant. His business is to sell cakes, not to give directions. We get into an arcade where a money changer in a turtleneck tells us to retrace our steps and turn left. He offers to pay me two pounds on the dollar over the official rate. I take the trouble to tell him how virtuous I feel about this sort of thing, and he cannot conceal his opinion, which is that I am very stupid. True. If I were *thinking*, I wouldn't say such things to a man whose trade is money. But there you are —the fellow with the dollars is frequently foolish. That —and here my thoughts also touch the case of poor Father Hoade, who went to Rome and died there—is life. We make our way out of the arcade and inquire of a stout, unshaven storekeeper in Arab headdress and busted shoes who deals in chipped green glassware. He lights up at our question. Yes, of course, *he* knows. Engaging us in conversation, he offers us coffee. Next he submits to our admiring inspection a crumbled snapshot in color of his son who is studying medicine in Chicago. I tell him that I am from Chicago. He is enchanted. The photograph, smudged by loving thumbprints, passes from hand to hand. So now we are bound together in friendship. The small dead end where we stand has the customary fallout of orange peel and excrement, eggshells and bottle tops.

Almost embracing us with his guiding arms, the shop-keeper escorts us to the Hamam. And here is the place itself at the corner, down a salmon-colored plaster passage that bulges asymmetrically. If this is Ladies' Day, we will have to turn back. Respectful of ladies' modesty, our friend opens the door cautiously and holds up a hand in warning. He inquires, shouting into hollow spaces, and then waves us forward. We enter a vast, domed, circular room that is perhaps a thousand years old—one thousand four hundred, our guide insists. For reasons of self-respect I am obliged to cut him down by a few centuries. But who can care for long about the dates. The little idiocy of skeptical revision passes off. I find myself to my joy in an ancient beautiful hot sour-smelling chamber. Divans made up with clouts and old sheets are ranged against the walls for the relaxing clients. Tattered towels hang drying on lines overhead. These lines crisscross up, up, up into dim galleries. An Arab woman, very old, is resting on a divan. One of her short legs is extended. She makes a gesture of Oriental courtesy. In this towel-bannered chamber people rest from the fatigues of bathing. We go through several steaming rooms, now empty. Our Arab friend says, "You spend a whole night here, you will be a very different man." I can well believe it. An attendant is scrubbing the floors with a stiff brush. He must be the husband of the ancient odalisque. He is stout, low, bandy-legged, and round-backed. He is so bent that if his deep-brown eyes, the eyes of a walrus, are to meet yours he must look upward. The white stubble and his color—the high color of a man of heat and vapor—are agreeable. "This is not the place I had in mind. The one I wanted to show you is much older," says Kahn. But I rejoice greatly in this one and ask for nothing better. As we leave, the old woman is conversing with one of her friends, an immense woman and deliciously fat, who has seated herself on the very edge of the sofa. On the cold cobblestones we say good-by, thanking the shopkeeper with the busted shoes. He goes back to his dark green glassware. "I suppose we must give up on the still older bath," says Kahn. He compensates himself by telling me about Max Nordau.

CHAIM Gouri, a poet and journalist, a strong-looking man in his early fifties, a head of black curls over a good square lined face—*une bonne gueule*. A turtleneck of forest green. He tells of a Peugeot belonging to an influential Arab family looted by Israeli soldiers during the Six Day War. Gouri took it from the soldiers and returned it. He was thanked by the Arab family and later invited to dinner by the lady of the house. "I am grateful for the car," she said, "but after you gave it back to us some of your soldiers came and took from me the jewels my mother had given me on my wedding day." Gouri promised to do what he could to help. As he did so he saw a Dutch woman, one of the dinner guests, grinning at him across the table. Later this woman explained why the incident had amused her so. "When the war broke out," she said, "we in Amsterdam began to store food and clothing for the Jewish refugees we expected to receive. After all, the Arabs threatened to wipe you out. It would not have surprised us if hundreds of thousands of new refugees had arrived in Western Europe. And here is a woman who complains that her bangles were taken. And you apologize to her. We in Holland had German soldiers entering our houses. The Germans themselves had Russians. . . ."

Nevertheless, Gouri's relations with this Arab family continued to be helpful. He was asked to help recover a certain family property, a house near the Jaffa Gate. He believed that he had made friends, so that when a French journalist asked Gouri to introduce him to an Arab fam-

66

ily he arranged an invitation to dinner. At the dinner table the daughter of the house, a grown woman, spoke her mind. Courageously, although Gouri said that she was trembling, she declared, "We will never accept the presence of Jews in our land." Gouri was shocked by this.

I didn't say what I was thinking, but the matter was clear enough to me as an American and also as a Jew. He wished to influence these Arab friends of his by his goodness. The idea is to clean things up, to feed the hungry, to build schools and hospitals, to hire workers at high prices to which they are unaccustomed, to give back looted cars and necklaces, and thus to win all hearts. But these Arabs play the old Alsace-Lorraine game, with Israel in the role of Prussia and themselves quavering bravely, like the old schoolteacher in Daudet's patriotic story, *Vive la France!*

I described Gouri as having "*une bonne gueule*" because he is, like Shahar, a Francophile. He knows no English. We have been speaking French more or less correctly, in high gear. Now he asks for my opinion of the French attitude toward his country. He describes visiting French intellectuals, Michel Butor among them, who reveal (rather than confess) that they know nothing at all about Israel. He wonders whether I can explain this strange ignorance.

I give him my view: France is a country whose thinkers, sitting in Paris, feel they know all that they need to know about the world outside. That outside world is what they declare it to be. If you want to know about the Australian Bushman, you look him up in Larousse. Standard works published in France contain, like Keats's Truth and Beauty, all that is known or needs to be known. Paris, for centuries the center of European civilization, grew rich in collective representations, in the indispensable images or views by which the civilized world conceived of itself. France was to such representations what British banking was to money. British banking is now close to ruin, but the image-of-the-world-as-seen-from-its-Parisian-center, fortified by the addition of a kind of Marxism, is as strong as ever in France. That is why French visitors strike Israelis as incomprehensibly incurious and ignorant. To wind up our conversation: much of Western Europe believes that capitalism is done for and that liberal democracy is perishing. If France cared anything about liberal democracy, about freedom, it would behave differently toward Israel, which alone represents freedom in the Middle East. But it prefers Arab feudalism, Arab socialism, Chinese communism. It prefers doing business with the Third World. It prefers anything to Israel.

JUSTICE Haim Cohn, when he fell in love with a woman who had been divorced and wanted to marry her, had to apply to rabbinical authorities for permission. This was denied because a Cohen, one of the hereditary high priests, cannot marry a woman who has been divorced. Then, since a high priest must be physically unblemished, Justice Cohn proposed to mutilate himself in a symbolic fashion—he offered to have one joint of his little finger surgically removed. But he was told that even if he cut off an arm he would remain a Cohen still. Justice Cohn, who represented Israel in the U.N. Human Rights Commission and went to America often, therefore married the lady in a civil ceremony in New York. Certain of the Cohns' friends thought it improper for a public servant to be so disrespectful to the rabbis, and Justice Cohn and his wife, yielding to their opinion, were married again by a Conservative rabbi. This rabbi was rebuked by his colleagues and had a hard time of it. So Justice Cohn told me. He is a big man and he looks taciturn, but you find that he has actually told you a great deal within a short time. Another paradox—at dinner he seems to be brooding on grim questions but you come away feeling that you've had a most cheerful time. Mrs. Cohn, a musicologist, is a large, impulsive, dramatic woman of considerable charm. The Justice was obliged to explain to his colleagues of the Human Rights Commission why a Cohen had to leave Israel in order to marry a divorcée.

I talked to Professor Werblowsky about his book on Joseph Karo, an impressive work about the great lawyer and the author of the *Shulchan Arukh*. Karo also left to posterity a personal record called *Maggid Mesharim*. The Maggid was a spirit that spoke "in silence and solitude" to the rationalist Karo—a voice within his mind. Maggidism, in the sixteenth and seventeenth centuries, was widely accepted by Cabalists, who believed that demons entered men and troubled them, but that angels too might enter a man and speak words of wisdom with him ". . . and when thou awakest after having fallen asleep amid thoughts of the Mishnah . . . and thy lips will vibrate. . . I am the Mishnah that speaketh in your mouth. The *Shekhinah* speaketh to you. . . ." Over drinks I asked the ingenious Professor Werblowsky, a slender, handsome man, whether he himself believed in the voice of the Mishnah in the mind or direct communications from the divine spirit. As a historian of religions he took it seriously, but he was himself a rationalist. Eventually such phenomena would yield to rational investigation. I should have guessed that this lissome, pin-striped professor with a carnation in his buttonhole and a fresh complexion to match would take the modern approach. Going back to his book, I found that he was indeed a modern professor, who spoke of Karo's Maggid as the manifestation of "a peculiar technique of spontaneously producing discursive intellectual, even highly specialized theoretical and speculative material without any conscious effort of thought." A professor's dream—a steady flow of discourse at the highest level! What other gift would an angel bring to an intellectual? Talk—wonderful inspiring, profound talk.

Alexandra and I gladly accept an invitation to a Sabbath dinner with the Werblowskys. The blessings and prayers are elaborate. I have never heard anything as elegant as Professor Werblowsky's Sephardic Hebrew. Three adolescent children, two daughters and a son, wait on us under the supervision of their mother. The Professor, in patriarchal style, is served first. His wife, pleased with all he does, all he says, visibly dotes on him—a rare sight this, in an age of embattled women. Yet who could fail to share the pleasure the soft and gentle Mrs. Werblowsky takes in her husband as he lounges in his large chair, presiding over the table?

My own heart must have a feudal compartment. I have a weakness for hierarchy. I remember how impressed I was in Tokyo when I spent a day with the Sumo wrestlers in their establishment. The Sumo Masters, immense and good-humored, glowing with vital power, their black hair pinned shining at the back of the head, sat before the cauldrons dishing out boiling stew to the disciples, who squatted about them in a circle and were served in order of rank. The Master with one hand could clutch the strongest of them by the head and pitch him out of the Sumo ring. That incomparable arm, pitted with acupunctures near the joints, was stirring the stew of weeds, fish, soybean curds, and nameless invertebrates, strangely aromatic and delicious. In his hand the ladle looked no bigger than a doll's teaspoon.

I think that Professor Werblowsky does not enjoy the ceremonious Sabbath meal more than I do myself. He reminds me (and he is not, of course, responsible for the odd thoughts that pass through my head), of a certain Jackie, a small boy in first grade in Montreal's Devonshire Grammar School, who once made me ecstatic with surprise by eating a plum during class. He took it from his schoolbag. He shined it first on his short pants; then, happy with the plum, happy with his foresight in bringing

a plum, happy with himself, he bit into it. This was my
discovery of talent. What an ingenious, original, and
striking idea it was to eat a plum in class. He was pleased
and he carried me with him. I, too, was delighted. So it
was with Professor Werblowsky. So it was, rather, with
my irrepressible but welcome association.

But the point of the evening, and we had many such
evenings in Jerusalem, was that no Orthodox family observed the Sabbath more fully than the Werblowskys. I
have since read a lecture by Professor Werblowsky, "Le
Shabbat dans la Conscience Juive." He refers to the Sabbath as "the precious gift of which the Talmud speaks."
But he adds, "I am using here the traditional language of
theologians, not my own."

There are many Israelis who do not believe, but there
are few who have no religious life. Life for the irreligious
in Israel is quasi-religious. After all, the Jews are in
Jerusalem not only because they are Zionists. There are
other reasons, and some of these reasons are indirectly or
in some degree religious. Such injustices as have been
committed against the Arabs can be more readily justified by Judaism, by the whole of Jewish history, than by
Zionism alone.

WENT walking with Dennis Silk. I had been reading his poems and marionette plays. They had stirred me, and I was in an agreeable state, keen to see the sights. We entered the Old City by the Damascus Gate and went ambling down the vaulted alleyways. I find the dirt of the bazaar delicious. I am pleased when I see donkeys backing out of bedrooms or bedroom-workshop-kitchens, or bakeries or basket-weaving establishments. In the alleys, tailors work away on the foot pedals of old Singer sewing machines. I rather like the tourist trash here dangling on strings in the doorways: necklaces, souvenirs, clay lamps, belts, sheepskins, and empty hassocks (you take them home and stuff them yourself), fleece-lined slippers, bush-ranger hats, antique brassware, and battered pieces of everything laid out on the ground—a scavenger's heaven. And Arabs with kaffiyehs tied with braided cord sucking at the narghiles in corners.

Dennis takes me to a gambling establishment in a coffeehouse, where people are slapping down big playing cards and shooting pocket billiards. The felt is patched with Band-Aids and there is no cue ball—the three shoots the nine, and the five bangs the fourteen. The players are young, dark, slender, and unsmiling.

We go to a body-building establishment near the Via Dolorosa. I call it a body-building establishment for it can hardly be described as a gymnasium, and yet bodies are being built. The walls are not exactly walls but rather hollows, bulges within a larger structure. The space is occupied by an immense collection of unclassifiable objects. In the entry there is an office which is also a concierge's lodge. From here a broad old man in a beret directs a multitude of activities. Small Arab boys are wiggling the knobs of a mechanical soccer game. Ranks of metal players kick at a steel ball, hardly more than a pellet. In a small alcove beside this, under an electric bulb a raw chicken lies beheaded and waits for dinner, its skin covered with a deathly moisture. Next, a room for athletes. The walls are covered with photographs of strong men in leotards and leopard skins. Some stand alone, exhibiting their shoulders, thighs, and arms. Some are surrounded by admiring families. It is not exactly clear to me how with such biceps you can embrace your dear ones. Barbells, dumbbells, and chest developers with springs take up most of the space. Two adolescent boys are nailing leather soles to the floor to give a footing to the weight lifters. They take a serious and highly professional attitude toward their work. In the last room of all, young men are working with the barbells. The barbells rest upon two supports near the top of the table. The young men lie on their backs and work their way upward into the lifting position. These weight lifters, fully clothed and wearing sweaters, perform the press exercise with desperate earnestness. I recall a muscle-building book called *How to Get Strong and How to Stay So,* with group photographs of champions of the 1890s, mustachioed and dressed in tights—the same look of solemnity and dedication. In this tiny room the young men take turns and press until they can press no more.

From this packing-case gymnasium we go to visit a settlement that adjoins the roof of the Church of the Holy Sepulcher. Ascending a broken stone staircase, you reach a parapet and come down again a few steps to a sunken floor beside the dome, where you see tall people standing beside low dwellings. In the December damp a black man in black garments approaches. He is a member of the tiny Ethiopian sect that lives in these cabins and has certain traditional rights in the Holy Sepulcher below. It is now evening and wet; wandering about, we find a narrow staircase and go down. Dennis explains that about a hundred and ten years ago the Coptic rivals of this sect managed to change the locks on the doors that gave direct access to the church courtyard, so that for more than a century these black men have had to take the long way around. It was not until the Six Day War that the Ethiopians had the locks changed and their doors were restored to them. They have two small chapels with holy pictures—fairly primitive—and bands of crimson, green, and yellow painted on the walls, portraits of patriarchs with white beards and staring eyes. From the shadows, priests in round black hats materialize. Centuries ago they took hold here and cling somehow to the side of this sacred place.

COMEDIES in which cries are torn from the heart
—*Così Fan Tutte, The Marriage of Figaro,*
Sterne's *Sentimental Journey;* I am drawn to
these, always, and to the Stendhals and Rossinis who carried Mozart and Sterne into the nineteenth century. From
this comes my affection for Samuel Butler—for the Butler at any rate who told in *The Way of All Flesh* how
three sisters played cards to decide which of them was
to marry the Reverend Pontifex. Perhaps Jung was right
in saying that the psyche of each of us was rooted in an
earlier age. I sometimes think that my own sense of fun
is nearer 1776 than 1976.

From the *International Herald Tribune,* a twentieth-
century note: Poor Thornton Wilder would have shud-
dered at his obituary. "Expressing the attitude of thousands of readers, Mrs. Lyndon Johnson said that he had
succeeded in making 'the commonplaces of living yield
the gaiety, the wonder and the vault of human adventure.' "

What the hell is this vault?

These Southern ladies sure know how to perfume a
phrase.

CERTAIN oddities about Israel: Because people think so hard here, and so much, and because of the length and depth of their history, this sliver of a country sometimes seems quite large. Some dimension of mind seems to extend into space.

To live again in Jerusalem—that is almost like the restoration of the Temple. But no one is at ease in Zion. No one can be. The world crisis is added to the crisis of the state, and both are added to the problems of domestic life. It is increasingly difficult to earn adequate wages, since from the first Israel adopted the living standards of the West. Taxes are steep and still rising, the Israeli pound is dropping. The government has begun to impose austerity measures. We meet people who work at two jobs and even this moonlighting is insufficient. The Israelis complain but they will accept the austerity measures. They know that they must, they are at bottom common-sensical. Yet everyone looks much shabbier and more harassed than in 1970.

In almost every apartment house the neighbors tell you of a war widow who is trying to bring up her children. The treatment of young widows and of parents who have lost their sons is, I am told, a new psychiatric specialty. Israel is pressed, it is a suffering country. People feel the pressures of enemies as perhaps the psalmists felt them, and sometimes seem ready to cry out, "Break their teeth, O God, in their mouth." Still, almost everyone is reasonable and tolerant, and rancor against the Arabs is rare. These are not weak, melting people. Only one sometimes hears on a mild day, by the sea or in the orchards, or when the mountains of Moab draw near in clear light, the wry Yiddish saying: "One could live, but they simply won't let you." On this speck of land—an infinitesimal fraction of the surrounding territories—a troubled people has come to rest, but rest is impossible. They often ask themselves why anti-Semitism should be so mysteriously pervasive. Even the Chinese, who know little of Jews, are Israel's enemies. Jews, yes, have a multitude of faults, but they have not given up on the old virtues. (Are there new ones? If so, what are they?) But at this uneasy hour the civilized world seems tired of its civilization, and tired also of the Jews. It wants to hear no more about survival. But there are the Jews, again at the edge of annihilation and as insistent as ever, demanding to know what the conscience of the world intends to do. I understand that Golda Meir, after the October War, put the question to her Socialist colleagues of Western Europe: Were they serious about socialism? If they were indeed serious, how could they abandon the only Socialist democracy in the Middle East? And the "civilized world," or the twentieth-century ruins of that world to which so many Jews gave their admiration and devotion between, say, 1789 and 1933 (the date of Hitler's coming to power), has grown sick of the ideals Israel asks it to respect. These ideals were knocked to the ground by Fascist Italy, by Russia, and by Germany. The Holocaust may even be seen as a deliberate lesson or project in philosophical redefinition: "You religious and enlightened people, you Christians, Jews, and Humanists, you believers in freedom, dignity, and enlightenment—you think that you know what a human being is. We will show you what he is, and what you are. Look at our camps and crematoria and see if you can bring your hearts to care about these millions."

And it is obvious that the humanistic civilized moral imagination is inadequate. Confronted with such a "metaphysical" demonstration, it despairs and declines from despair into lethargy and sleep.

JAY Bushinsky of the Chicago *Daily News* is stable and solid; he has a round, sensible, attractive face. As we sit chatting in the lobby of the new Hilton Hotel, he tells me that some time ago he was allowed by the Israeli authorities to cover a military operation. A minute island in the Red Sea was raided, the Egyptian garrison taken by surprise. Bushinsky saw a sentry who had been cut down by machine-gun fire. "He was a young boy," said Bushinsky. "Shot in the leg. Flesh hanging in tatters. Bleeding to death. I said to the commanding officer, 'Can't we do something for him?' and he said, 'First things first,' so we went on. And he was right. I never saw the kid again. It stays with me."

Bushinsky and I had met on the Golan Heights in 1967 when I was *Newsday*'s correspondent. When he reminded me of this I told him that David Halberstam, a real correspondent, had made fun of my dispatches, saying that I ran up large Telex bills to describe to Long Island readers the look of a battlefield. In self-defense I asked Halberstam for his definition of real journalism. "When an Egyptian general and his entire army were captured," said Halberstam, "and a newspaperman asked him why not a shot had been fired, he answered that firing a shot would have given away his position." And *that*, in Halberstam's view, was one of the most brilliant stories filed in the 1967 war.

The point of view is, uncontestably, professional. I wondered, however, whether there weren't other legitimate viewpoints, and I raised the matter with Bushinsky.

I learned that he, a seasoned newspaperman, was vulnerable, too. He couldn't get out his mind the memory of an Egyptian boy's mangled leg.

I had never seen a battlefield before 1967 and at first didn't understand what I was looking at. Riding through the Sinai Desert, I thought it odd that so many canvas or burlap sacks should have fallen from passing trucks. I soon realized that these bursting brown sacks were corpses. Then I smelled them. Then I saw vultures feeding, and dogs or jackals. Then suddenly there was an Egyptian trench with many corpses leaning on parapets and putrefying, bare limbs baking in the sun like meat and a stink like rotting cardboard. The corpses first swelled, ballooned, then burst their uniform seams. They trickled away; eyes liquefied, ran from the sockets; and the skull quickly came through the face.

Some readers, I thought, might wish to know what the aftermath of battle is like.

Y, an Israeli novelist, tells me how, in 1948, when he was only seventeen, he lay all day feigning death among the dead in a field near Jerusalem. The Jordanians had trapped his company and wiped it out. They were dug in on the hillsides and fired on anyone who looked alive. The vultures came, said Y, and began to feed. They began with the eyes always. Y lay there and the birds did not touch him but fluttered near and he heard them, the soft ripping sound that they made. He lay there until dark.

Y is married to a tall American woman whose face is small and wonderfully beautiful. She is very thin and her movements are very slow. When she rises from her seat her unfolding seems endless—she has more joints than a carpenter's rule. Her speech is slow, she falters. She looks and sounds a bit otherworldly, a strange American nursery child. She and Y live in a poor Arab quarter. They take in sick children, old cripples, hurt animals. Nola Auerbach, John's wife, went to visit her one day and found that she had put an ailing donkey in her bed and was tending it. At times her eccentricities make her seem a bit crazy, but on examination she proves to be not crazy but good. We've come to believe that passionate intensity is all on the side of wickedness. Mrs. Y looks a bit like Virginia Woolf. Also like an autistic child I knew in Paris in 1948.

Y is convinced that Israel has sinned too much, that it has become too corrupt, and that it has lost its moral capital and has nothing to fight with.

ON a kibbutz.

Lucky is Nola's dog. John's dog is Mississippi. But John loves Lucky too, and Nola dotes on Mississippi. And then there are the children—one daughter in the army, and a younger child who still sleeps in the kibbutz dormitory. Lucky is a woolly brown dog, old and nervous. His master was killed in the Golan. When there is a sonic boom over the kibbutz, the dog rushes out, growling. He seems to remember the falling bombs. He is too feeble to bark, too old to run, his teeth are bad, his eyes under the brown fringe are dull, and he is clotted under the tail. Mississippi is a big, long-legged, short-haired, brown-and-white, clever, lively, affectionate, and greedy animal. She is a "child dog"—sits in your lap, puts a paw on your arm when you reach for a tidbit to get it for herself. Since she weighs fifty pounds or more she is not welcome in my lap, but she sits on John and Nola and on the guests—those who permit it. She is winsome but also flatulent. She eats too many sweets but is good company, a wonderful listener and conversationalist; she growls and snuffles when you speak directly to her. She "sings" along with the record player. The Auerbachs are proud of this musical yelping.

In the morning we hear the news in Hebrew and then again on the BBC. We eat an Israeli breakfast of fried eggs, sliced cheese, cucumbers, olives, green onions, tomatoes, and little salt fish. Bread is toasted on the coal-oil heater. The dogs have learned the trick of the door and bang in and out. Between the rows of small kibbutz dwellings the lawns are ragged but very green. Light and warmth come from the sea. Under the kibbutz lie the ruins of Herod's Caesarea. There are Roman fragments everywhere. Marble columns in the grasses. Fallen capitals make garden seats. You have only to prod the ground to find fragments of pottery, bits of statuary, a pair of dancing satyr legs. John's tightly packed bookshelves are fringed with such relics. On the crowded desk stands a framed photograph of the dead son, with a small beard like John's, smiling with John's own warmth.

We walk in the citrus groves after breakfast, taking Mississippi with us (John is seldom without her); the soil is kept loose and soft among the trees, the leaves are glossy, the ground itself is fragrant. Many of the trees are still unharvested and bending, tangerines and lemons as dense as stars. "Oh that I were an orenge tree/That busie plant!" wrote George Herbert. To put forth such leaves, to be hung with oranges, to be a blessing—one feels the temptation of this on such a morning and I even feel a fibrous woodiness entering my arms as I consider it. You want to take root and stay forever in the most temperate and blue of temperate places. John mourns his son, he always mourns his son, but he is also smiling in the sunlight.

In the exporting of oranges there is competition from the North African countries and from Spain. "We are very idealistic here, but when we read about frosts in Spain we're glad as hell," John says.

All this was once dune land. Soil had to be carted in and mixed with the sand. Many years of digging and tending made these orchards. Relaxing, breathing freely, you feel what a wonderful place has been created here, a homeplace for body and soul; then you remember that on the beaches there are armed patrols. It is always possible that terrorists may come in rubber dinghies that cannot be detected by radar. They entered Tel Aviv itself in March 1975 and seized a hotel at the seashore. People were murdered. John keeps an Uzi in his bedroom cupboard. Nola scoffs at this. "We'd both be dead before you could reach your gun," she says. Cheerful Nola laughs. An expressive woman—she uses her forearm to wave away John's preparations. "Sometimes he does the drill and I time him to see how long it takes to jump out of bed, open the cupboard, get the gun, put in the clip, and turn around. They'd mow us down before he could get a foot on the floor."

Mississippi is part of the alarm system. "She'd bark," says John.

Just now Mississippi is racing through the orchards, nose to the ground. The air is sweet, and the sun like a mild alcohol makes you yearn for good things. You rest under a tree and eat tangerines, only slightly heavy-hearted.

From the oranges we go to the banana groves. The green bananas are tied up in plastic tunics. The great banana flower hangs groundward like the sexual organ of a stallion. The long leaves resemble manes. After two years the ground has to be plowed up and lie fallow. Groves are planted elsewhere—more hard labor. "You noticed before," says John, "that some of the orange trees were withered. Their roots get into Roman ruins and they die. Some years ago, while we were plowing, we turned up an entire Roman street."

He takes me to the Herodian Hippodrome. American archeologists have dug out some of the old walls. We look down into the diggings, where labels flutter from every stratum. There are more potsherds than soil in these bluffs—the broken jugs of the slaves who raised the walls two thousand years ago. At the center of the Hippodrome, a long, graceful ellipse, is a fallen monolith weighing many tons. We sit under fig trees on the slope while Mississippi runs through the high smooth grass. The wind is soft and works the grass gracefully. It makes white air courses in the green.

Whenever John ships out he takes the dog for company. He had enough of solitude when he sailed on German ships under forged papers. He does not like to be alone. Now and again he was under suspicion. A German officer who sensed that he was Jewish threatened to turn him in, but one night when the ship was only hours out of Danzig she struck a mine and went down, the officer with her. John himself was pulled from the sea by his mates. Once he waited in a line of nude men whom a German doctor, a woman, was examining for venereal disease. In that lineup he alone was circumcised. He came before the woman and was examined; she looked into his face and she let him live.

John and I go back through the orange groves. There are large weasels living in the bushy growth along the pipeline. We see a pair of them at a distance in the road. They could easily do for Mississippi. She is luckily far off. We sit under a pine on the hilltop and look out to sea where a freighter moves slowly toward Ashkelon. Nearer to shore, a trawler chuffs. The kibbutz does little fishing now. Off the Egyptian coast, John has been shot at, and not long ago several members of the kibbutz were thrown illegally into jail by the Turks, accused of fishing in Turkish waters. Twenty people gave false testimony. They could have had a thousand witnesses. It took three months to get these men released. A lawyer was found who knew the judge. His itemized bill came to ten thousand dollars—five for the judge, five for himself.

Enough of this sweet sun and the transparent blue-green. We turn our backs on it to have a drink before lunch. Kibbutzniks ride by on clumsy old bikes. They wear cloth caps and pedal slowly; their day starts at six. Plain-looking working people from the tile factory and from the barn steer toward the dining hall. The kibbutzniks are a mixed group. There is one lone Orthodox Jew, who has no congregation to pray with. There are several older gentiles, one a Spaniard, one a Scandinavian, who married Jewish women and settled here. The Spaniard, an anarchist, plans to return to Spain now that Franco has died. One member of the kibbutz is a financial wizard, another was a high-ranking army officer who for obscure reasons fell into disgrace. The dusty tarmac path we follow winds through the settlement. Beside the

undistinguished houses stand red poinsettias. Here, too,
lie Roman relics. Then we come upon a basketball court,
and then the rusty tracks of a children's choo-choo, and
then the separate quarters for young women of eighteen,
and a museum of antiquities, and a recreation hall. A
strong odor of cattle comes from the feeding lot. I tell
John that Gurdjiev had Katherine Mansfield resting in the
stable at Fontainebleau, claiming that the cows' breath
would cure her tuberculosis. John loves to hear such bits
of literary history. We go into his house and Mississippi
climbs into his lap while we drink Russian vodka. "We
could live with those bastards if they limited themselves
to making this Stolichnaya."

These words put an end to the peaceful morning. At
the north there swells up the Russian menace. With arms
from Russia and Europe, the PLO and other Arab militants and the right-wing Christians are now destroying
Lebanon. The Syrians have involved themselves; in the
eyes of the Syrians, Israel is Syrian land. Suddenly this
temperate Mediterranean day and the orange groves and
the workers steering their bikes and the children's playground flutter like illustrated paper. What is there to keep
them from blowing away?

MOSHE the masseur is delicate in person; his hands, however, have the strength that purity of purpose can give. He arrives cold from the street in his overcoat, which is bald in places. He is both priestlike and boyish, a middle-aged idealistic Canadian. He seems untouched by life. When people say "untouched by life," they often mean that one has—not always for praiseworthy reasons—lived on the whole without cynicism. He is fresh, he is somewhat adolescent at fifty. He believes in his work. He has a vocation. He was born to relieve people of their muscular tensions. He talks to you about exercise, breathing, posture, about sleeping with or without pillows, with open windows or shut. None of this is small talk, because he holds the body sacred. His face is ruddy, his nose slightly bent, his expression tender. I find in him the clean-living Scout's-honor innocence of the boys I knew who worked out at the YMCA and, still wet from the showers, darted into the street when the thermometer stood at ten below. Moshe comes from Montreal and studied massage under a French master. Moshe speaks French a bit, Canadian style. His master taught that the body must be treated with the deepest respect. "You don't pick up an arm as though it was a separate piece of something. You've seen *Jaws*? You saw that fellow's leg when it sank all by itself when the shark bit him. Well, no arm and no leg should ever be treated as if detached. No real masseur will fling you around. For me, massage is a personal relationship and kind of an act of love," explains Moshe. He is fra-

gile but holds himself straight; he is intensely sincere.
Catching himself too late, he says that, considering my
age, I am in good condition. He teaches me to do push-
ups while I rest my weight only on the fingertips. He also
shows me how to relieve a stiff neck by tracing the numbers from one to nine with my head. He makes his own
mixtures of almond and olive and wintergreen oils. He
takes off his shoes and sits behind me on the couch to
snap my vertebrae into place. He is respectful, profes-
sionally impersonal, personally full of concern for your
bones and muscles, and his conversation is highly in-
formative. He knows a lot about Jerusalem. He knows
army life, too, for he served as a medic in 1967 and
again in 1973 in the Sinai Desert. He tells me what he
saw and describes some of the wounds he dressed. He
tells me also, faltering a bit, about wounded enemy
soldiers for whom there was no transportation. He asks
me to make a moral judgment. I taste again the peculiar
flavor of that green unripe morality of naïve people, of
middle-aged North American adolescents—for which no
adult substitute has been found. Do the senior members
of the class really know the answers to these hard questions?

IN an obscure journal, an article by Professor Tzvi Lamm of the Hebrew University charges that Israel has lost touch with reality.* Lamm's view is that although the Zionist idea in its early stages seemed more dreamlike than practical, it was soberly realistic. Its leaders knew just how much power they had—or had not— and adhered closely to their goals. They were not hypnotized and paralyzed by their own slogans. Jewish leadership, and with it Israel as a whole, later became "autistic." Autism is defined by Lamm as "the rejection of actual reality and its replacement by a reality which is a product of wish-fulfillment." The victory of 1967 was the principal cause of this autism. Israelis began to speak of the West Bank of the Jordan as "liberated" territory. "The capture of lands aroused . . . a deep, sincere, emotional response to the territories . . . and to the historical events that took place in them: the graves of our patriarchs and matriarchs, paths along which the prophets once trod, hills for which the kings fought. But feelings cut off from present reality do not serve as a faithful guideline to a confused policy. This break with reality did not necessarily blind men to the fact that the territories were populated by Arabs, but it kept them from understanding that our settlement and taking possession of the territories would turn our existence as a state into a powerful pressure that would unite the Arab world and

*"Zionism's Path from Realism to Autism: The Price of Losing Touch with Reality," *Dispersion and Unity* 21/22, Jerusalem, 1973–74.

aggravate our insecure situation in a way previously unknown in our history."

Zionism, Professor Lamm argues, is different from other kinds of nineteenth-century nationalism in that it did not originate in order to bring people back to a national homeland. "It arose in order to establish sovereignty, and hence a national home, for Jews without a home . . . it was a rescue movement to save a people in a critical situation by concentrating it within one territory, and allowing it to take its political fate in its own hands." Lamm admits the importance of God's Covenant, of the Promised Land, the Holy Land, Eretz Yisrael, in inspiring the Jews to auto-emancipation. But with success the emphasis shifted; the need to save the Jews was translated into something else—the project of "redeeming the land." The early Zionist leaders were trying to redeem the people. Realistic Zionist leadership was willing to accept partition "in order to absorb and save Jews rather than to remain faithful to slogans that it itself had coined." Rescue is the true aim of Zionism—not the "liberation" of the Promised Land but the rescue of the Jews, repeatedly threatened with annihilation. But Lamm believes that Ben-Gurion had a messianic character. "Ethnocentrism," or a national "narcissism," appeared in Israel. By 1956 it had become aggressively opportunistic. It attached itself imprudently to the expelled, decayed powers, France and England, "without any consideration for the future." It relied upon military force and followed the politics of "hiring out our sword" instead of seeking a peace settlement with Egypt. It ceased to think of itself as the sanctuary for rescued people but began to think of a State, with an Army. The effects of the Sinai campaign were, first, to unify the Arab world against Israel and, second, to bring the Arab-Israel dispute into global politics. The Suez War of 1956 consolidated the power of Nasser and the cabal of Egyptian colonels and more definitely turned the Egyptian masses, who now connected the Jews with the old imperialists, against Israel.

It was after the Six Day War, according to Lamm, that autism began to prevail over realism. All at once the Israelis were arguing about demography, about getting the Arabs to emigrate, "about keeping Israeli citizenship from the Arabs who would remain," about rebuilding the Temple. But what did they say about peace? Some said, writes Professor Lamm, that "in exchange for peace we would grant the Arabs—peace." The Zionist movement had rejected policies of "positions of strength." A national coalition without definite policies governed the country. Ideological leadership was abandoned; a "business-minded leadership" took over. Statesmen, thinkers, writers, journalists became proud, lost sight of the true reason for the founding of the state—the "rescue" reason —and became power-intoxicated, deluded. The nation, according to Professor Lamm, now lived in a dream world; political debate virtually ended. The Yom Kippur attack was "a blow to the minds of a public doped with empty slogans, living in a fog, and avoiding reality."

Harder words follow. In the Six Day War Israel conquered and occupied Egyptian, Syrian, and Jordanian territories. Does it mean to keep them? In 1939 England and France had gone to war with Nazi Germany because they could not accept its expansionism, its policy of territorial conquest and annexation. What was wrong for Germany cannot be right for Israel. The comparison may seem harsh, and Lamm does not go so far as to equate Israel with Nazi Germany. What he does argue is that Israel has for many years demanded that the Arab world recognize a legitimate Jewish claim to Eretz Yisrael, but Israel did not, after the Six Day War, declare that it recognized the rights of a Palestinian entity. The Rabin government has recently begun to concede—or, at least, to hint at the concession of—rights to the Palestinians.

I am mildly scolded by Israel Galili, minister without portfolio in the present government, for being ignorant of the government's Arab policy. I have tried to learn what this policy is, I say. When I arrived in Jerusalem, I obtained a mass of government literature on the subject, but from it no clear picture emerges. I know that the government will not negotiate with the PLO. I know also that it refused to tolerate a Palestinian state on the West Bank, between Amman and Jerusalem. But that is not all, says Mr. Galili. He is a small, solid, keen man with tufts of Ben-Gurionesque white hair and pale but not faded blue eyes. He sizes me up, quite rightly, as an interested inexpert observer. He glances at Shimon Peres, the defense minister, who is present, as if to say, "You see? They hardly ever know what they're talking about." Then he explains that Mr. Rabin has explicitly recognized the existence of legitimate Palestinian grievances. (I should, perhaps, make it clear that we are lunching at the Mishkenot Sha'ananim and that Mayor Teddy Kollek is present.) I repeat that I have read what the government information service has to say on the matter but see no sign that Palestinian grievances are officially recognized. "Then we are very poor in public relations," says Mr. Galili. That is true enough.

At this point Teddy Kollek observes that the older leaders have never been willing to acknowledge an Arab problem. Golda Meir flatly rejected its existence. Mr. Galili, an old Zionist and kibbutznik, disputes Kollek's observation. Mr. Peres is too superior a politician to be drawn into a dispute of this nature over lunch. He has really come to discuss literature with me, a fellow writer. And there is a vast distance between the Zionist idealists Professor Lamm talks about and the political subtlety of Mr. Peres. Mr. Peres carries an aura. The shine of power is about him. I have observed this before. It was visible in the late Kennedys, Jack and Bobby. They were like creatures on a diet of organ meats—of liver, kidneys, and potent glands. Their hair shone, their coloring was rich, their teeth were strong. I assume this to be the effect of wealth and power, not of the eating of giblets or cod's roe, for Leopold Bloom, who ate these with relish, did not dazzle Dublin with his vitality.

But I continue with Professor Lamm's argument. What has happened to the old ideals of Zionism, he asks. Settlement of the land was considered by the pioneers not only as a political act but "as the daring creation of a new social, cultural, national" life. The attacks of thieves, bandits, and "pogromists" made self-defense necessary. But that was very different from what is happening now. Now settlers go into "liberated territories" like colonialists, with army support, and take land from the "natives." Lamm names Pitchat Rafiach, the Jordan Valley, the Golan Heights, and Kiryat Arba as places where this has occurred. In its realistic period, Zionism took itself to be the movement of a remnant. Hitler very nearly succeeded in destroying European Jewry. To the survivors, Israel meant life. It did not mean political power. "The time has come to abandon the deceptive notion that we are a 'power' in the region and the overbearing self-righteousness of our 'historical rights' to the land," Lamm writes.

He has few illusions. Even the most realistic policies will not guarantee survival. The enemies of Israel are terrible. "The forces opposite us are seeking to destroy us: the moderates, politically; and the extremists, physically. Anyone who does not admit this . . . is nothing but a dreamer." Israel must come to a settlement with these enemies. If that is not possible, then "we have little chance of continuing to exist in this land. In comparison with the forces that we must muster, the potential military, political, and economic forces of our opponents . . . are beyond all measure." The idea that Israel may prevail by force becomes a nightmare. Professor Lamm calls for a return to political realism. The historical attachment of the Jews to Israel is intense, but so is the feeling of the Arab nationalists; so is the competition between Russia and the West in the region; there is also the matter of the petro-dollars and the flow of oil. "If we are lucky, we have not yet spoiled the chance to return to the situation of a society living with reality, fighting for its existence and directed by leaders who dare to stand before it with a political position," he concludes.

One of the oddities of life in this country: when someone says "the struggle for existence," he means literally that. With us such expressions are metaphorical. Nor is the word "nightmare" adequate. On television the other night, people in Beirut were murdered before my eyes. Palestinians under siege shot down two of their own comrades, prisoners who had been sent by their Christian captors to ask for a truce. And these are not fictions that we see on the box but frightful realities—"historical events," instantaneous history. Survivors of the Nazi concentration camps tell us they preferred their worst nightmares to the realities of the morning. They embraced their most frightful dreams and clung to them.

The very Orthodox Professor Harold Fisch, bearded and wearing a skullcap, tells me that "the liberated territories" must be colonized and reclaimed by the Jews. The West Bank is Promised Land. For that matter the East Bank is too. Professor Fisch, English by birth and dean of something or other at the new university in Beersheba, has no patience with the objections I offer. He tells me fiercely in his Oxbridge voice that we American Jews are not Jews at all. It is a strange experience to hear such a judgment in such an accent. "You will say," he adds, "that we may be annihilated by the Arabs in reclaiming our land according to God's promise. But history sometimes gives us no choice. It is shallow to argue with one's fate. If this be our fate as a people we must prepare to accept it."

THE famous Institute at Rehovoth, one of the world's greatest centers of scientific research, bears the name of Chaim Weizmann, the first President of Israel, but it is the child of Meyer Weisgal. Weisgal says he is no scholar, though he was for many years the editor of a Zionist magazine. Yet he was the planner, the builder, the fund raiser, the organizer, and the directing spirit of this place. Early visitors who saw nothing here but sand, heard nothing but the jackals whimpering, were taken by Weisgal to the top of a dune and told, "We will have physics here, and biology there, and chemistry around the corner." Now Weisgal has his guests chauffeured through the gardens he has created and says, "So we put chemistry in that group, and the physicists over there, and so on. And now let me show you the beautiful memorial we built for Weizmann himself." His intimacy with Weizmann appears to be unbroken by death. He speaks of him continually.

I see the old boy in Jerusalem. As we climb an endless flight of stone stairs in the warm sun Weisgal stops and says, "I'm now eighty-one. Eighty-one is not eighteen, you know." His shrewd brows tilt upward. His white hair spreads outward from the widow's peak, going wide at the back. A bit winded, he continues to climb in his dressy chesterfield with its velvet collar. He gets himself up wonderfully. His suit is elegantly made. His necktie must be a Hermès. He has aged greatly since we last met ten years ago. I had been taken aback by his handshake: had I never noticed that his hand was mutilated? Two of his fin-

95

gers have been amputated. His face is as clever and energetic as ever. His nose swells out, intricately fleshy, grainy —a topographical sort of nose. He is recognizably what people in the twenties called "an old sport," "a good-time Charlie"—one of those men in broad-brimmed fedoras who took drawing rooms on the Twentieth Century Limited in the John Barrymore days, people who knew headwaiters and appreciated well-turned-out women. There were many Jews of this sort, big butter-and-egg men who made and lost fortunes. My late friend Pascal Covici, the publisher, was one of these. Pat knew how to order a fine dinner, how long to let wine breathe, how to cherish a pretty woman, how to dart into the street and stop a cab by whistling on his fingers, how to negotiate a tough contract—not so tough, perhaps, since he paid out too many advances and lost his shirt. These Weisgals and Covicis came over in the early years of the century from Poland or from Rumania and were inspired by America, fell in love with it. Weisgal at thirteen years of age sold matches and papers in the streets. In 1917 he was a doughboy. Covici raised grapefruit in Florida in 1919, then, after failing as a fruitgrower, opened a bookshop near City Hall, in Chicago. America seems to have instilled a certain boyishness in these old guys, an adolescent candor and gaiety, a love of plain talk. They had, in that generation, no patience with bunk. Weisgal became a great fund raiser; he knew how to talk to millionaires.

A niggardly millionaire from whom he had expected a large gift to the Institute reluctantly took out his checkbook after he had been entertained at lunch and wrote a check for twenty-five thousand dollars. "Thanks a lot," said Weisgal, "but the meal has already been paid for." He tore the check up. In the 1920s he would have lighted his cigar with it. Weisgal knows that he operates in the old style. He spoofs himself as he recalls old times with Max Reinhardt, hambone money-raising spectaculars in the Manhattan Opera House. The Jewish journalist and man-about-town is one of the deep ones, strangely disguised. The diligent man of Solomon's proverb might stand before kings; Weisgal, who is diligent, has done more than stand before them. He knows how to charm the rich and get large sums out of them; he knows how to interest the great. Great men have taken him very seriously. On the walls of his house in Rehovoth are photographs of himself and his wife, Shirley, and their guests and acquaintances—scientists, bankers, and American Presidents. Shirley Weisgal talks in a matter-of-fact way about them. It made Einstein uncomfortable to wear shoes. Oppenheimer openly wept at dinner; he prophesied that a growing number of young American scientists would flee the spiritual vacancy of America and come to work here.

But Weisgal the Zionist pioneer misses the United States. Just now on the stairs of Jerusalem stone he stops again, unwillingly, to catch his breath. Then he says, "Next week I go back to the States. I'm looking forward to that." Then he takes off the vicuña coat with the velvet collar and hangs it over his frail shoulders: "But it's no good kidding. I can't get around the way I used to," he says. The sun shines on his strong nose and on the rippled white hair that fans out stiff and wide beyond the clever occiput. "Stern is waiting up there for me. This is bad planning, all these stairs. Well, here goes, again." We are climbing to the new studio Teddy Kollek has had a part in building above the Mishkenot Sha'ananim. The violinists Isaac Stern and Alexander Schneider are holding auditions. Dozens of children, many of them recent immigrants from Russia, come daily to play for them. The fiddle culture of the Heifetzes and the Elmans is still strong among the Russian Jews (a death-defying act on four taut strings by means of which you save your life). Stern's visits to Israel are by no means holidays; he works very hard in Jerusalem. He and Weisgal are organizing something. Stern has told me that he has appealed to the authorities on behalf of soldier-musicians. The hands of a violinist who does not play for months on end may lose some of their skill. The damage can be permanent. "He's always into something," says Weisgal. "I don't lead a restful life myself."

Weisgal flies to New York soon. From New York he will go to California and from there to Florida. He will speak to hundreds of people. The Institute needs millions of dollars. No need to tell him he's overdoing things, he knows that quite well. He's not a carpet-slipper type. "I may conk out any time," he says. But it óccurs to me as we toil upward that dying isn't what he has in mind. He wants to blow into New York again and talk to physicists and philanthropists, and see his sons and grandchildren, and eat delicious dinners and hear good jokes, and to do there what probably no one else can do for the Weizmann Institute and for Israel. As for conking out, he must think of that, certainly. But I remember what Harold Rosenberg said to me one day when I asked him how he felt about his approaching seventieth birthday, "Well, sure, I've heard about old age and death and all those things, but so far as I'm concerned it's all a rumor."

THE children in the Master Class come forward
with their fiddles and take positions before Stern
and Schneider. A twelve-year-old boy comes forward. He is small, dark, muscular, concentrated. He
tucks the violin under his chin, rises on his toes, closes
his eyes, dilates his nostrils, and begins to play the Mendelssohn Violin Concerto in E. For a long time now, I've
disliked it. I'm down on all this silvery whickering. It depresses me. I associate the Mendelssohn concerto with
bad Sunday afternoons, with family dinners, suppressed
longings, domestic captivity, and boring symphony
broadcasts. Yet as soon as the kid begins to play, there
are tears in my eyes. This is idiocy. This small Russian
boy is putting me on. The rapt soul et cetera is a trick.
I try to smile at his fiddler's affectations but my face
refuses to obey. I can only think, How did I ever learn
to smile such a cheap smile. I'm well rid of it, then, and
I sit listening. For five minutes, this boy reconciles me
even to the detested Mendelssohn.

SIGHTSEEING with two poets, Harold Schimmel and Dennis Silk, in the Old City. It's not proper sightseeing, though. I do not, like a good tourist, carry a camera. I've never liked cameras, and I haven't owned one since 1940. In that year I photographed some long-legged pigs in Mexico, on the island of Janitzio in Lake Pátzcuaro. I'd never seen such stilted pigs, and they were well worth snapping. The camera came from a hock-shop on South State Street and there were small holes in the bellows, so that my pigs were speckled white.

Schimmel, a student at Cornell in the days when Vladimir Nabokov taught there, did graduate work at Brandeis with Philip Rahv. He has learned Hebrew well enough to write in the language. I feel, with these two, that I'm on a holiday, briefly relieved of the weight of politics. Big Silk has an outcurved profile, a fine bent nose, and his delicate ways amuse me. He becomes absorbed in a display of Persian bottles, his eyes go wide, his underlip comes forward, he moons, and we have to bring him away. Schimmel takes us to a shop specializing in old picture postcards—Allenby's arrival in Jerusalem in the Great War is commemorated in every shade of brown. There are also lacy greeting cards, tons of them; and scribblers; and Greek editions of Zane Grey, for the proprietor is an old Greek gentleman. He has an immense stock of stereopticon slides, and maps, and photographs going back to the last century of patriarchs and pilgrims, and faces from the Ottoman Empire. Great Turkish or Balkan mustachios such as these soldiers and statesmen wear were still common in Chicago in the twenties. One saw them on South Halsted Street, near Hull House, in coffeehouses and candy stores. The men who drove the gaudy white-and-scarlet waffle wagons and announced themselves to the children with bugle calls were rich in such whiskers. (Waffles, half-baked, gluey, and dusted with powdered sugar, a penny each.) We shuffle through the cards, looking for something exceptional. Elias Canetti, an excellent novelist and somewhat eccentric psychologist, argues somewhere that a passion for antiquities shows us to be cannibals, if not ghouls. The cards are the dark yellow of muscatel grapes, but otherwise suggest nothing edible. I pick up a pre-Hitler German picture of Jews praying at the Western Wall. Silk, who is a collector, digs under piles of trash while the Greek proprietor makes us what is evidently a set speech on the great Hellenic tradition of liberty, sounding off about Miltiades and Pericles as if they lived just down the street.

Schimmel and Silk are looking for the weavers' alley. What they find instead is a big stone stable, once part of a princely establishment. The carved ornaments, all blackened, go back to the fourteenth century, so we are told by two friendly young Arabs who are tinkering with machinery here. Oh, yes, the stable is still used, but the donkeys and mules are out for the day. Dennis Silk sensitively interrogates the young men. They speak Hebrew well enough to give information. The information is for me, of course. Silk thinks I take a normal tourist's interest in all of this. It doesn't matter to me whether the stable goes back to the fourteenth or to the sixteenth century. What interests me is that one of the young men now decides his feet need washing. He hikes up his trousers and squats, grinning to himself—both these Arabs find us amusing—and pours water from a green bottle over his toes, balancing himself ably on one foot. He has what I call cavalry legs, short and full. A woman, too, may have the cavalry leg; it does not prevent her from being shapely.

We never do find the looms. Perhaps the weavers have taken a holiday. We buy round sesame buns and, at an Arab stall stuffed with luxuries, cans of Portuguese skinless sardines in a spicy sauce, and some cucumbers, and we go to Silk's house for lunch. Silk lives in no-man's-land amid the vacant lots. The house just beyond his was a Jordanian outpost before 1967, and coming home at night was risky in prewar days, especially if one had been drinking, for it wasn't altogether clear where the boundaries were. The lots are safe enough now. There are goats and dogs and cats, and decaying buildings that would have been splendid during the Mandate, and weeds and cans and bottles, and a beautiful view of the mountains of Moab in their tawny nakedness. A sharp little bitch trots with us. She must have a litter somewhere near, for she's so full of milk her udders touch the ground. When Silk opens the door, she enters. "Is that your pet, Dennis?" I ask. He says, seriously and sadly, "No, she's not. But she was a dear friend of my dog, who died last month, and she still comes looking for him."

There are not many comforts in Dennis's house. I can't decide whether it's a hut or a cabin. The property belongs to the Greek Orthodox Church and Dennis goes in person to pay the rent three times a year dealing with a strange functionary—part lawyer, part bookkeeper—who always tries to get the better of his poet-tenant. "It's very Oriental," says Dennis. "You can't just put down your money and ask for the receipt. You have to drink coffee and fence back and forth and go through all the Levantine tricks."

Books and pictures fill the two rooms. Dennis is not a tidy bachelor; he doesn't mind a bit of dust in the place. There's all the difference in the world between vile dirt and poet's dirt. I understand why his windows aren't washed; washing them would make a glare and spoil the tone entirely. This place is perfect as it is—a batik bedspread on the mattress, lots of manuscripts with coffee rings on them. We could do with a little heat, but it isn't essential, the vodka will warm us. Israeli vodka is very good. So is the slivovitz, raki, and tzuika—even the aquavit here is drinkable. Dennis rolls open the sardine cans, puts out cheese and buns and bottles. Papers and books are not removed from the table, only pushed aside, and we eat and drink. We talk about writers. In a journal lying on the floor is one of Gore Vidal's interviews. I always read these with pleasure. It's curious, says Vidal in this one, how full of concepts American speech is: "Americans continually euphemize; they can never call anything by its name. . . . You never say what you mean; this is not good for character." We have become the most pleonastic, bombastic people in the world and, furthermore, a nation of liars. I add to this that no people has ever had such a passion for self-criticism. We accuse ourselves of everything, are forever under horrible indictments, on trial, and raving out the most improbable confessions. And all for world consumption. It's true that we lie a great deal—Vidal is right about that—we lie like mad. There are no Tartuffes in our literature, no monster hypocrites, no deep cynics. What we have in their place is a great many virtuous myths that we apply to our lives with imbecile earnestness. Everything bad is done for the best of reasons. How can a man like Richard Nixon think ill of himself? His entire life was a perfect display of *Saturday Evening Post* covers. He was honest, he had healthy thoughts, went to meeting three times each Sunday, worked his way through school, served his country, uncovered Communist plots. It is impossible that he should be impure. Moral accountancy in America is a fascinating subject. The blaming, too, is fascinating. People seem to become more American in sharing the blame for offenses they cannot have committed. The descendants of East European immigrants had no share in the crime of slavery, yet they insist that it was "we" who were responsible. What I see in this is a kind of social climbing. My friend Herbert McClosky, a political scientist, perfers to interpret it as moral ambitiousness: a people that expects everything of itself blames itself for everything. I believe that these confessions of national failure and guilt are also a form of communion. "We are what we get high on," said Jerry Rubin in *Do It!* Anyway, nothing makes us happier than to talk about ourselves. Our own experience as a people has become a source of ecstasy. And here am I, doing it, too.

Schimmel and Silk lead the conversation back to poetry and poets. What was Ted Roethke like? Well, he was a round-faced blond giant—a bit like Silk, come to think of it. He liked to take off his shoes and his jacket and turn his waistband outward to ease his belly. When he played tennis at Yaddo, in Saratoga Springs, his volleys tore down the net. I have become a compendium of such information. And yet I never intended to remember any of it. But it amuses Silk and Schimmel, and there is a bottle on the table, and the disorder of Silk's rooms reminds me of Greenwich Village thirty or forty years ago. Silk, who admires John Berryman and wrote an excellent article on the *Dream Songs,* asks me whether I can read the poems in Berryman's own manner. I can try, I say; I heard them from him often enough, in Minneapolis and elsewhere. John would sometimes telephone at three in the morning to say, "I've just written something delicious! Listen!" So I know well enough how he recited his songs. I read some of my favorites to Silk and Schimmel. Drink and poetry and feeling for a dead friend, and the short December afternoon deepening by the moment from a steady blue to a darker, more trembling blue—when I stop I feel that I have caught a chill. Silk no more minds the cold than a walrus minds the ice.

The poets walk me back to Sir Moses Montefiore's windmill. I tell them, "It's been super." And so it has. "When I came to Jerusalem I thought to take it easy. But no one takes it easy here. This is the first easy day I've enjoyed in a month."

The mill is one of the landmarks of the New City. Teddy Kollek has had soil brought and old olive trees and cypresses planted, making a considerable park along

King David Road. Near the mill, the coach of Sir Moses
Montefiore is on display and tourists and schoolchildren
are brought here and lectured on the history of the
quarter. Sir Moses, as indefatigable as Kollek himself
(although in his portraits the old philanthropist looks to
be a more dreamy man than the mayor), induced some
of the Jews to leave their squalid quarter and settle outside the city walls. This was a difficult undertaking.
Palestine in the mid-nineteenth century was not the most
orderly part of the Ottoman Empire. Settlers and travelers
were attacked by brigands and murderers, but old Sir
Moses eventually succeeded and the Jews formed a settlement on the far side of the Gai-Hinnom, facing the walls
of the city and Mount Zion. Dennis has written a curious,
half-imaginary account of Montefiore and his pilgrimages
and projects. Now the mill and the renovated buildings
have been gilded with historical glamour, and the buses
bring sixth graders and foreign rubbernecks all day long,
and there are brass plaques on the walls. The mill has
something in common with Chicago's Water Tower.
When Mrs. O'Leary's cow kicked over the lantern and
Chicago was destroyed, almost nothing survived the
flames except the knobby Victorian-Gothic Presbyterian-
looking stone tower that stands on Michigan Avenue
like the pet of the surrounding skyscrapers, a piece of
history—or of history, commerce, and promotion.

And in Jerusalem it is politically important that Sir
Moses and his coach and mill should be worked into
history. Mayor Teddy Kollek neglects no opportunity to
emphasize the legitimacy of Jewish claims in Jerusalem.
There is no deceit in this. The claims *are* legitimate. Yet
I often feel that Kollek is too aware that he has a limited
time to make his case before the tribunal of world opinion. Sometimes it is hard to distinguish between his personal energy and the urgency of the need. But here is
the windmill, a monument to the stout dreamer Sir Moses,
with his beard, and boots, and the British top hat on
his Jewish head; and here are the kids and the tourists
and the teachers and the guides. Often they lecture loudly

at our very doorstep, in front of the Mishkenot Sha'-
ananim.

On my way home, feeling the vodka I've drunk with
Silk and Schimmel, I pass through the tourists' lines.
But I've just had a holiday with two poets. They released me from weeks of preoccupation with the merci-
less problems—the butcher problems of politics. The mind
took a different route today. It isn't that one escapes
suffering along this route. I couldn't help grieving over
Berryman's suicide, when I recited some of his *Dream
Songs,* but it wasn't senseless grief. Something else
mingled with the feelings of heaviness. The transforming
additive: the gift of poetry. You think yourself full of
truth when you've had a few drinks. I am thinking that
some of the politicians I meet are admirable, intelligent
men of strong character. But in them the marvelous
additive is lacking. It is perhaps astonishing that they
aren't demented by the butcher problems, by the insen-
sate pressure of crisis.

I am fascinated by the profusion and ingenuity of Jewish ideas on the future of Israel. Thinking of them, I picture bin after architect's bin filled with blueprints and projected details. I have a letter from Mikhail Agursky, a Russian writer who recently came to Jerusalem. What he tells me is that "the Jews can be productive and efficient if one very strange condition is fulfilled—that their objectives ought to be strictly unrealistic from a current point of view. If they pursue such objectives they are out of competition. Zionism," he goes on, "can be revitalized now only by an injection of such nonrealist objectives. Personally I am advocating such an objective —to make Israel the center of the new civilization (not less!), taking into consideration the evident decline of the Western (and Eastern as well) civilization. . . . Pragmatically only such ideas can be successful for the Jews."

I find a résumé of an article by Agursky on Russian immigrants in Israel in a recent number of *Insight,* a small paper edited by Emanuel Litvinoff and published in London.* What the essay assumes—that Russia will presently permit the mass emigration of its Jews—is far from certain. The Soviet government, thoroughly anti-Semitic—it has twice broken relations with Israel, and there is no other country it denounces so roughly—is not about to supply Israel with what it needs most. The population problem, everyone agrees (and in a country

*"Soviet Emigration and Israel's Future," *Insight,* October 1975.

in which unanimity is rare), is one of Israel's most serious problems. Thousands are leaving. Are they being replaced? Reliable figures are hard to come by. When the impressive defense minister, Shimon Peres, expressed the hope that large numbers of Russian Jews might soon be coming, he diminished his impressiveness somewhat. A military leader ought not to sound so wistful. Israel's casualties in 1973 have been terribly damaging; some suggest that its losses were comparable to those that bled the British in World War I, advancing the view that in the Somme and other great battles British power was cracked and England hurt beyond recovery. Is it likely that the Russians do not understand how serious Israel's 1973 losses were and that they will allow the country to recover its strength by the mass immigration of Russian Jews?

But Agursky assumes that Russian Jews will soon be pouring in and believes that they can change the character of Israeli society and alter the fate of the world. According to Agursky, as *Insight* paraphrases his statement, Soviet Jews who joined the Zionist movement "had an idealistic image of Israel as a society united by feelings of brotherhood and solidarity." They believed that Jewish moral traditions had assumed secular forms here, and that a nonreligious Jewish population would manifest a Jewish awareness or a binding Jewish moral element. In this, they made a serious error. Here it is the national and religious heritage that matters. Jewish history makes no sense, Agursky says, without the actual source of Jewish integrity and persistence. A Jewish state summoned into existence cannot replace this peculiar compound, and the common opinion that Israel can exist only under the Western system of democracy "is a profound mistake which can cost our people its life." Western democracy is now "on the brink of catastrophe." Democracy can endure only when a free people is capable of self-discipline and refrains voluntarily from weakening the political order. In the West enough of the old religious morality remains to preserve the parliamentary system. "Precisely for this reason, totalitarianism in all its forms, when striving to undermine the Western world, seeks first and foremost to destroy those institutional forms that are dictated by religious values. The main aim of totalitarianism is the undermining of religious education, traditional ways of life and the family, and complete liquidation of moral censorship." By such means, totalitarianism aggravates the sickness of Western democracies. But if the West is near collapse, so is the totalitarian world.

Agursky believes that Israel should place its confidence in traditional and religious values. As matters now stand, it is a sense of the common danger and not a religious feeling of brotherhood that unites Israeli society.

The Russian Jews, he concludes, can make an important contribution to the necessary revival of religious feeling. Their totalitarian experience has matured their souls as well as toughened their minds. Bitter experience has given them a wisdom too scarce to be wasted. Perhaps Agursky also means that what sections of the Western world seem to long for—peace and justice in a Communist society—these Eastern Jews already know.

Agursky's argument makes me think of Henry Fairlie's book *The Spoiled Child of the Western World: The Miscarriage of the American Idea in Our Time.* America, in Fairlie's view, is no longer preoccupied with the struggle for existence. He sees a new sort of permissiveness recommended by fashionable Existentialism. Since the struggle for existence "ceased to be a problem, one's existence in itself became the problem. Existentialism is not a philosophy for someone who lacks a crust of bread."

If the struggle for existence has indeed slackened in America and a major phase of history has ended, we need not wonder at the strange looks we receive from a world astonished at our privileged state and appalled by our lightheartedness and light-headedness. Agursky wonders whether democratic America has enough self-discipline to pull through. Many writers have pointed out that in world history liberty is an exceptional condition. Rulers are not inclined to share their powers with the ruled. Periods of liberty have been very brief. Our species knows little about being free. Ruskin, writing of Thucydides' *History,* says that his subject was "the central tragedy of all the world, the suicide of Greece." Possibly we are once more at a suicidal point, and this is what Russian dissidents, people who have managed by heroic resistance to keep mind and judgment intact, are thinking when they consider our behavior.

But to finish with Agursky: he speaks of an older revolutionary generation which has not been forgotten, and of the messianic universalism of that generation and its desire for social justice. He thinks that the Hebrew prophets in Russian translation should be put into the hands of the new immigrants from the Soviet Union "to enrich their national awareness," according to the paraphrase in *Insight.* "No capital investment could be as effective as this spiritual investment." Agursky himself writes, "Israel must become the centre of a new civilization as was dreamed by the prophets, the best representatives of the Jewish people." The editor of *Insight* comments that Russian Jewish intellectuals of Agursky's type have begun to ask questions "that Western Jews had long thought answered" and "were coming up with different results. Sometimes they sounded naïve, more often powerful and arresting."

Knowledge of evil such as these Russians have acquired cannot be without its side effects. Their understanding of Western capitalism was acquired in Russia. So they think us frivolous and our condition chaotic. They hold the prevailing European and Russian view of our waywardness. To them we present a danger to freedom. But they are immensely hopeful, too. Israel the center of a new civilization? I can see what Agursky means when he counsels us not to be too realistic. He advocates— But no, no, I don't want to level serious arguments at Agursky. He is too beguiling. What I like about these Russian dissidents—the Solzhenitsyns and the

Sinyavskys as well as the Agurskys—is their wakefulness. By contrast we seem very drowsy.

With us in the West wakefulness, for some mysterious reason, comes and goes. Our understanding fires up briefly but invariably fades again. Sometimes I suspect that I am myself under a frightful hypnotic influence—I do and do not know the evils of our times. I experience or suffer this alternate glowing and fading in my own person, and I see that others, too, are subject to it. I am familiar with the history of World War I and of the Russian Revolution. I know Auschwitz and the Gulag, Biafra and Bangladesh, Buenos Aires and Beirut, but when I come back to facts anew I find myself losing focus. Then I begin against reason to suspect the influence of a diffusing power—a demonic will that opposes our understanding. I am forced to consider whether Western Europe and the United States may not be under the influence of a great evil, whether we do not go about lightly chloroformed.

It is reported in the papers that the American Embassy in Moscow suspects it is being exposed to microwave radiation. According to the UPI, experts speculate that the Russians intend the radiation to activate microphones hidden in the embassy building, to interfere with American jamming devices, or "according to a more sinister report, the radiation was designed to induce lethargy in American diplomats." This may be a total delusion, which the public seems willing to share with the experts.

But the Russians, if they really knew it, need no such lethargy-inducing devices. The free countries are curiously lethargic about their freedom. The credit of revolution is strong in Western Europe, while capitalism, especially in its hated American form, is held to be dying. Many exult over its approaching death. Tired of old evils, they long for "the new thing" and will not be happy until they've had it. Baudelaire writes, in one of his journals, that life is a hospital in which each patient believes that he will recover if he is moved to another bed. When

I lived in Paris in the late forties, I became an involuntary student of this subject. I learned from shopkeepers, *garagistes,* barbers, waiters, concierges that "revolutionary" ideas (bed-changing ideas), now thoroughly banal, had reached all levels of French society. Anticipating the coming victory of communism, the bed that would cure all old evils, many French intellectuals prepared themselves opportunistically for careers in the new regime. The leaders of French thought had three decades in which to teach their countrymen the facts about Russia and Eastern Europe. These can be summed up in a few words: there is no free society in Eastern Europe; communism has thus far created only police states. One may reply that freedom is less important than equality, security, and the welfare of the working class. I've heard such replies given. These days they are given often by Indian intellectuals, who justify the repressive measures adopted by Indira Gandhi. In helping to interpret this, political theorists are less useful than mythologists and demonologists.

In our apartment in the Mishkenot Sha'ananim, the sideboard, the deep marble windowsills, the coffee table, the desk are covered with papers, journals, pamphlets, and books on the Middle East. The night staff in the lobby watches TV. The chief guard with his round cropped head and big eyes is an Oriental Jew, slender and dark. A gun is tucked into the waistband of his dungarees. Coming home at night to the books and papers, you meet armed patrols. You see them on the road above and in the gardens below.

MESSAGES arrive continually from Mayor Teddy Kollek. He invites Alexandra and me to a concert, to visit an archaeological site, to have tea with the Greek Patriarch. He thinks of everything, never fails to consult you, remind you, thank you. His punctilious notes make me feel like a boor. Kollek is ponderous but moves quickly—a furiously active man. His is a hurtling, not a philosophical soul. His face does not rest passively on its jowls; its creases are those of a shrewd man. His nose is straight, short, thick, and commanding; his color is ruddy; his reddish hair falls forward when he goes into action. Balzac would have taken to the mayor. Kollek is to Jerusalem what Old Goriot was to daughters, what Cousin Pons was to art objects. But no category will hold a phenomenon of such force. On duty (he is never really off), he bangs about the city in his car. He takes you on a tour of the new suburbs he has built in East Jerusalem. He arrives in the yellow bus belonging to the municipality, with several assistants (horticultural, sanitary, recreational), to show you the parks he has created in vacant lots everywhere. There is even a park for the blind, with Braille tablets to describe the view and the plants. A gardener himself, he seems to know every bush in the city. Besides which he knows the donors. Computerlike, he retrieves the names of philanthropists and his secretary writes them down. "We can fit a little playground into that space. Let's send So-and-So a letter about that." Kollek's acquaintance is international; he knows the rich, the great, and the glamorous

113

everywhere. He is a bit like Meyer Weisgal in this respect. Everyone serves his ends, and no one seems harmed by such serving. Kollek has a talent for speaking bluntly—his blue eyes plainly tell you that—but he observes formalities nevertheless. He turns a fine phrase, is a man of some culture. His manners are Viennese, with super-added British graces. He is fluent in English and speaks it with a slightly British accent. When he entertains scholarly English guests, he is expansively happy. With Sir Isaiah Berlin one day, he was in heaven. He gave him a glorious lunch that amounted to a banquet and made a learned pun on Kant and Königsberg. His memoirs, should he ever find time to write them, will fascinate the world. He had few kind words for Golda Meir's autobiography, recently published. A disappointing work. I agree with him. Mrs. Meir, a woman of powerful character, seems to have censored her strongest feelings and in her book has adopted the American congressional-courtesy style—"the distinguished gentleman from the great State of Arkansas" kind of thing. Her motive is evidently political. Still thoroughly identified with the government of Israel, Golda Meir does not wish to give offense or make enemies among its American supporters. Her kind words about President Nixon and others are probably sincere, but she is stingy with her readers and does not give them what she might have given. One digs under these compliments in vain, trying to learn what her deeper feelings are. I doubt that Kollek will impose similar restrictions on himself. A force of nature, without coaxing he makes his feelings clear.

In good weather, Kollek hurries about the city in Israeli style, shirt open at the throat. In December you may see him in a fur hat, with a knotted muffler, his vest buttoned, but never in an overcoat, for he moves fast and a coat would get in his way. Two elderly ladies told me how he had commandeered their taxicab. They had just asked the driver to take them to the Old City when a heavy stranger hurried out of the King David Hotel, sprang in beside the driver, and in a low peremptory voice gave him an address. One of the ladies was violently angry; the other laughed as she told me of the incident. "He didn't take us far out of the way," she said. The mayor was pressed for time and made no excuses. Kollek, who knows how to be extravagantly polite, can also be a bear. Still, few mayors anywhere in the world are so personally attentive to the needs of their constituents. Elderly Mr. Freudenthal, the proprietor of Graphos Stationery, told me that he was put out because the city, obliged to narrow the sidewalk, had blocked the entrance to his shop by installing a stoplight so near his door that customers had to sidle in. "I went to see the mayor about this," he said. "And what did the mayor do? He took his hat and came with me immediately to make an inspection. He agreed that it was terrible. He promised to move the traffic light." In this age of public relations, everyone is somewhat skeptical of such behavior. Worldliness demands that I be suspicious of Kollek. But I warn myself not to coarsen my perceptions. It's true that things are not what they seem. But things may disconcertingly become exactly what they seem. Mr. Freudenthal's request was met; the light was moved.

What is entirely genuine in Kollek, without admixture, is his love for Jerusalem. Not even his detractors deny it. Christians and Arabs may not accept the rule of Israel, but they are satisfied with the Kollek administration. I am told that without Arab votes Kollek would not have been re-elected. People jokingly speak of him as one of the Arab politicians. He is on excellent terms with Muslim religious leaders. They fare better with him than they did under Jordanian rule. Kollek loves to address churchmen by their appropriately honorific, sonorous titles. He says, "Your Beatitude," and his big face brightens with the relish of it. Echoes of the Austro-Hungarian Empire, probably—a feeling for tradition and hierarchy. Whatever it may be, Kollek delights in it. It makes his day to greet the aged Greek Patriarch. It does a lot for me, too, I must say. The Patriarch is ancient, densely bearded up to the eye sockets, faltering a little as he walks toward us. He kisses Kollek on both cheeks, and with warmth. He sits in a comfortable chair to the left of his throne. We are served coffee and seven-star Greek brandy. The conversation, in French and English, is lively. His Beatitude shows fatigue. He has just returned from a conference with a bishop in Amman. It seems that the Pope has proposed a single date for the observance of Easter by both churches, and the Greek bishop in Amman is ready to accept. The Patriarch appears uneasy lest the Roman Church come in the eyes of the world to stand as the single great representative of Christianity. There is a colored photograph of the Patriarch with the Pope, taken when the Pope visited Jerusalem. When the Patriarch makes a particularly strong point about these Easter arrangements, he turns toward the picture as if to see what effect his argument is having. Learning that Alexandra was born in the Greek faith, the Patriarch gives her a small gold cross. As he fastens it at the back of her neck, Kollek asks me, uneasily, "You don't mind that, do you?" Have I any objection to such a gift? Not at all. I am very amused by the scene, and not least by Kollek's concern for my religious sensibilities.

Like many thousands of Israelis, Kollek has intense and complex relations with the world outside. It seems to me often that life in this tiny country is a powerful stimulant but that only the devout are satisfied with what they can obtain within Israel's borders. The Israelis are great travelers. They need the world. When they feel the need—and they feel it often—they are obliged to go far. The neighboring Arab countries are forbidden to them. They fly to Europe or America. If they are not to fall behind, hematologists, mathematicians, sociologists must go into the world. But it is more than professional necessity that impels them. Love and fascination mingle with practical considerations. From the eighteenth century, European Jews, when revolution began to release them from their ghettos, hastened to enter modern society; they adored and hungered for it—its cities, its political life, its culture, its great men, its personal opportunities. Even the Holocaust did not destroy this attraction. And now, carrying Israeli passports, Germans or Poles no longer, they are nearly as eager and starry-eyed about the great world as their ancestors.

The extent of Kollek's international connections is fabulous. He knows the international corporations, the banks, the great universities, the political parties. He is in touch with Brazilians, Finns, Rhodesians, Washingtonians, Parisians. "Oh, Kim Roosevelt," he says, or "Oh, Joe Alsop." And also with Rothschilds and Warburgs, and even with Hapsburgs and Romanoffs, I imagine. These acquaintances are seldom superficial. He gives one reason to think that he knows backstairs, attics, and cupboards as well as salons and boardrooms. It would be hard for a parvenu name-dropper to surprise him with a new rumor. He beams when the gossip is good; he can generally add to it. One of my friends in the forties used to say, "When I do it, it's not gossip, it's social history." Yet in spite of the relish with which Kollek listens to social history he is a stainless idealist. He fights to preserve and expand and improve the city that holds the soul of his people.

The object of Kollek's extensive building program is evidently to make Israeli possession of the city a *fait accompli*. Under heavy pressure he holds his ground admirably. Though he commandeers a cab in the street and runs off with two elderly ladies, his power is far from absolute. Right-wing Jewish groups give him as many headaches as the meddling of international institutes, prestigious visiting firemen who damn him for disfiguring Jerusalem, or justice-loving Americans whose even-handedness can be so deadly. There are hideous new buildings in Jerusalem, it is true. Kollek is, I think, humiliated by them. The Wolfson Condominium is most unattractive. The multitudinous windows of the new Hilton look to me like the heavy-lidded eyes of insomnia sufferers, aching for rest. Kollek, supported by an international advisory committee, has resisted the developers and their architects. Nevertheless, he has sometimes had to yield to bankers and developers. Jerusalem has its eyesores, and there are some who see political and even military significance in the new structures. They say they are built like fortresses. Hugh Clayton in the London *Times* of June 25 lists nine new settlements in the Jerusalem area alone and adds that the Israeli government's Ministerial Settlement Committee is now considering proposals from the world Zionist organization for another seven of them. He says, "The United States Government has branded the settlements as illegal, and the chairman of the Ministerial Settlement Committee, Israel Galili, says he regrets the debate within the United States but expects it to continue, which seems to indicate that he does not believe American leaders will go beyond verbal opposition." It is not clear to me what view Kollek takes of Israel's settlement policies.

I can understand, on historical and psychological grounds (with some help from experts), the Muslim objections to a Jerusalem controlled by Israel. Christian attitudes can also be interpreted by a reasonable man determined to understand. Those who baffle me are the disinterested parties, themselves without religious beliefs, calling for this that or the other form of shared control, for a "free" city (I am old enough to remember the dismal history of the Free City of Danzig) or for a "neutral" Jerusalem. Jean-Paul Sartre, in one of his frequent interviews, favors the "neutral" position.

What would be the practical effect of such schemes, Kollek sometimes asks. You sit down to lunch with him; he virtuously orders a salad; then a dish of sweets in pleated papers is set down, and he eats them all. Jerusalem in 1967 was chaotic. In 1976 this ancient place offers all the services you can find in the neatest of modern municipalities. His impartiality is not seriously questioned; he has built apartment houses, kindergartens, and schools for Jews and Arabs alike. Kollek learns what the latest things are and brings them here. Plays are performed for Arab children who never saw a theater before. For the first time all the holy places are equally respected. Kollek is not so naïve as to expect gratitude and cooperation from the Arabs in return. For one thing, the Arab world would accuse grateful Arabs of betrayal, the extremists would mark them for punishment. And then he has been in politics long enough to understand that when people's daily needs are satisfied they are free to become ideological and to assert their independence in hostile acts. Still, I often think that Kollek wants to show the world, and especially the Arab world, what good sense and liberality can do; he wants to persuade everyone that what is feasible on a small scale can be done wholesale. Arab demands for self-rule in Jerusalem will eventually have to be taken into account. Kollek is certainly aware of this, and my guess is that he is prepared to consider reasonable proposals for a shared administration. The Arabs know that there is no meanness or arbitrariness in him. He has shown by his fairness that coexistence is possible and desirable. He is Israel's most valuable political asset.

Even in the last century the Jewish Quarter of Jerusalem was, by all accounts, one of the filthiest places on earth. The shambles was there; rats and dogs dug into the offal and fought; the city threw its garbage into the Jewish streets. This had been the practice for a long time. When the Arabs captured the city in the seventh century, Professor David Landes, of Harvard, writes that they "found the rock on top of Mount Moriah, the old site of the Temple, covered with tons of garbage, laboriously hauled up and dumped there by way of insult and desecration. The Arabs cleared the rock and built the beautiful Mosque that we now know as the Dome of the Rock or Mosque of Omar. But the shambles was maintained, a lasting plague to the Jews of Jerusalem."* Travelers like Pierre Loti were horrified by the Jews of Jerusalem, flittering batlike in their vaulted alleys. They must be perverse and wicked to deserve such a painful life, Loti felt.

*"Palestine Before the Zionists," *Commentary*, February 1976.

Here was evidence that they had, indeed, committed a great crime against the Redeemer who had arisen in their midst.

One no longer sees such Jews as Loti described. Kollek is building a new Jewish Quarter in the Old City. The principal relic of the ancient quarter is the ben-Zakkai synagogue, blown up by the Jordanians when they took over in 1948. Kollek does everything possible to avoid vengefulness. He is conciliatory, steadily reasonable. The cruel history of this city can have a stop, he seems to be saying. He is, in this respect, less a psychologist than a rationalist: how can people fail to recognize their own interests? What a Jewish question that is! Such an appeal to rational judgment attempts to go behind Arab history. I have been reading a document by Professor Yehoshafat Harkabi, of the Hebrew University, in which he suggests that Arab and Israeli scholars should cooperate in studying the conflict. "Perhaps this bespeaks an inordinate faith in the power of rationality," he says, "but I believe that this would be a step towards peace." Professor Harkabi informed me that his essay was published in Sartre's *Les Temps Modernes*. "It was published, too, in an Arabic translation in Tel Aviv," he writes, "but could not be distributed to the Arab countries."*

"An inordinate faith in the power of rationality"? The professor might better have called it Jewish faith or Jewish longing or even Jewish transcendentalism.

*"Position of Israel in the Israel-Arab Conflict," written in October 1965.

DOUBLE window shades don't keep out the morning light. It wakes me and I go to fill the kettle. Shade flowers grow in the long corridor of Mishkenot Sha'ananim. The kitchen window opens on a small garden—hardly that: a terrarium with glass walls, open at the top. The flowers are exotic birds-of-paradise, too flamboyant for my taste. The door stands open as we drink our tea, and we look across the Gai-Hinnom to Mount Zion. Shahar insists that the air of Jerusalem feeds the intellect—one of the great rabbis believed this—and he mentions the psalm in which the psalmist sings of God's garment of light. You can take this seriously in Jerusalem. A character in one of Isaac Bashevis Singer's extraordinary stories thinks, looking at the sky in Israel, "No, this isn't just an ordinary *khamsin* but a flame from Sinai. The sky above is not just atmosphere but a heaven with angels, seraphim, God." This is Jewish transcendentalism, too, in a very different part of the mind. With Singer it comes out as though a spring were pressed at the appropriate moments in a story. My inclination is to resist the imagination when it operates in this way. Yet, I, too, feel that the light of Jerusalem has purifying powers and filters the blood and the thoughts; I don't forbid myself the reflection that light may be the outer garment of God.

I go to the door and look toward the Judean Desert. I see not so much the terrain as the form of some huge being. Its hide is gray. The distant small buildings are gray also. Letting down the barriers of rationality, I feel that

I can *hear* Mount Zion as well as see it. I have explored
the hill. On the top is a church surrounded by scaffold-
ing, masons at work on the walls. There are certain
monastic buildings and many, many graves (the cellular
subsurface of the city is filled with bones). On the dusty
paths you see donkeys, occasionally a camel. The western part of the Old City's sixteenth-century wall comes
to an end in a narrow paved road. There is no reason
this hill should have a voice, emit a note audible only to
a man facing it across the valley. What is there to communicate? It must be that a world from which mystery
has been extirpated makes your modern heart ache and
increases suggestibility. In poetry you welcome such
suggestibility. When it erupts at the wrong time (in a
rational context) you send for the police; these psychological police drive out your criminal "animism." Your
respectable aridity is restored. Nevertheless, I will not
forget that I was communicated with.

I enter a flagstoned court in the Greek quarter and see
that it is covered by a grapevine. The single stem from
which this wide, rich arbor grows rises from a little pit
some feet below the pavement. Light shimmers through
the leaf cover. I want to go no farther that day. I had the
same feeling on a visit to the Armenian Church when the
old librarian showed me his collection of illuminated
manuscripts. He explained that under the floor of the
church was an ancient cistern, which provided exactly
the degree of humidity necessary for the preservation of
these relics. As then, I am tempted to sit down and stay
put for an aeon in the consummate mildness.

The origin of this desire is obvious—it comes from the
contrast between politics and peace. The slightest return
of beauty makes you aware how deep your social wounds
are, how painful it is to think continually of nothing but
aggression and defense, superpowers, diplomacy, terrorism, war. Such preoccupations shrink art to nothing.
They endanger even the more ordinary kinds of aesthetic
experience, the ability to react to what the philosopher
David Wight Prall (whom I read in a course given by

Eliseo Vivas in Wisconsin in 1937) called "aesthetic surfaces." Gore Vidal has noted in an interview the American weakness for nifty terms and I suppose I wouldn't be fully American if I didn't share it—hence "aesthetic surfaces." But Prall was speaking of ordinary life and common experiences, of a cup of coffee or the folds of a curtain, a bucket under the rain pipe: "Lingering, loving contemplation" of flavors, colors, shapes, fragrances. I believe that this ability to contemplate has also been damaged. This again brings to mind the observation of A. B. Yehoshua on the difficulty (the impossibility, rather) of screening out the great noise of modern life, "the lack of solitude, the inability to be alone in the spiritual sense, and to arrive at a life of intellectual creativity."

In the West, in America, we are not subject to such strain, but we too have mechanisms operating within, answering to more remote stimuli, phantoms of crisis that set off endless circuits of anxious calculation. What drives the soul into the public realm is, first, the reality of the threat to civilization and to our own existence; second, our duty to struggle and resist (as we conceive this); third, the influence of public discussion in the press, on television, in books, in lecture halls, or at dinner tables, in offices; and fourth, perhaps, is our own deep desire to send the soul into society. If this were in the higher sense political, there would be nothing to complain of. "With word and deed we insert ourselves into the human world," wrote Hannah Arendt in *The Human Condition,* "and this insertion is like a second birth." Man seeks immortality, she said. To realize this end he must affirm his identity through speech and action, and this is precisely where politics comes in. For it is the unique genius of politics that it "teaches men how to bring forth what is great and radiant. . . ."

But what I am thinking of is somewhat less Athenian. The material weight of life lies upon us more and more heavily. To Hannah Arendt such pressure is not genuinely political but social, economic. She may be right.

I am no theorist; I use the word "politics" broadly and mean by it everything in the public part of life. Thus technology is politics, money is politics, our common life in America is in its every aspect politics. It has become a passion with us—our social and national life with its parties and issues, our cities, our gun laws, our crime rates, our housing needs, our old-age problems, our interest rates, our position in the world, our sexual revolution, our racial revolution, our gasoline, our sports, our weather. This is certainly not political in a Greek sense, but what else are we to call it? Ruskin called it self-worship. He said that "general misgovernment" had created a vast populace in Europe, and in other continents a still vaster one, and that this populace existed in "worship of itself." It can "neither see anything beautiful around it, nor conceive anything virtuous above it; it has, toward all goodness and greatness, no other feelings than those of the lowest creatures—fear, hatred, or hunger...." One can take this seriously without complete agreement. For a great world population, what is lingering loving contemplation, what is art? Proust, who translated Ruskin into French, takes up this theme of politics and art in the novelist's indirect manner: on the one side, Bergotte Vinteuil, Swann's love of music; on the other, worldliness, snobbery, the Dreyfus affair, the Great War. Proust was still able to hold the balance. That was six decades ago.

I close the door on Mount Zion and go upstairs to the reception desk to get the morning papers. The Mishkenot is built on a slope, and the lobby is a floor above our apartment. Behind the desk stands Annie. She is a lovely, dark young woman, Moroccan by birth. She is not very happy these days. But dejection deepens her beauty. I wouldn't dream of telling her that. We exchange a few remarks. My old-fashioned French slang from the forties amuses her. Then she hands me the Jerusalem *Post* and the *International Herald Tribune*. I glance at the headlines, and a film comes between me and the light. My heart goes down an octave or more. I descend to the flat to see what has become of the Dutch hostages, the British hostages, and of the Lebanese, the Portuguese, the Angolans.

I am reading a book from which my attention never wanders: Lucy Vogel's *Aleksandr Blok: The Journey to Italy,* published in 1973. Blok writes of an episode in his journey: "I feel the need to share it with others. Why? It is not because I want to tell others something amusing about myself or have them hear something about me that I consider poetic, but because of something else—an intangible 'third force' that does not belong either to me or to others. It is this force which makes me see things the way I do and interpret all that happens from a particular perspective, and then describe it as only I know how. This third force is art. And I am not a free man, and although I am in the government service, my position is an illegal one, because I am not free; I serve art, that third force which from the world of outer reality brings me to another world, all its own—the world of art. Therefore, speaking as an artist I must inform you without attempting in any way to thrust my views on you (for in the world of art there is no such thing as pressure) that the descent underground and the mountain climb which I described have many features in common, if not with the process of creation, then at least with one of the modes of comprehending a work of art.

"The best preparation for attaining such understanding is to experience the sort of feeling which arises in the wanderer who suddenly finds himself in a forest clearing, in the land of the machaon butterflies, or beside an aqueduct at the foot of a mountain. I am not saying that this is the only method; there are others that are equally re-

liable: for example, to suffer great misfortunes or wrongs
in life, or to experience the deep physical fatigue that ac-
companies prolonged mental idleness. But these are ex-
treme alternatives, so to speak, and the first way is for
me the most natural and the most dependable. One can
achieve this through repeated efforts or through one's
own merits. But to work consistently at such an unusual
task is not easy for anyone in the rush of our civilization.
Everyone is in such a hurry nowadays." Blok wrote this
in 1909.

DR. Z, the gynecologist, came from Rumania at the age of sixty and at seventy-five is still working hard. She says that Israel's socialized medicine does not make her life easy. She examines more than sixty women daily. She occasionally persuades young men to marry their pregnant sweethearts. She comforts Jewish brides from the Arab countries who weep because they have been married two whole months and haven't yet conceived. At dark, closing her office, she toils up the stairs to her apartment and lies down. After a hard day she eats pistachio nuts. She insists they restore her.

One of Dr. Z's colleagues examined all seven children of a North African laborer. "I'm glad to say there's not a thing wrong with any of them," he reported. The father was incensed. "I didn't bring these kids to the doctor to be told there was nothing wrong. I brought them for treatment." He grabbed a chair and threatened the doctor with it, shouting, "Treat them!" The doctor gave placebos to everyone. His nurse urged him to prescribe a strong laxative for the father. "Serve him right!" she said. The doctor resisted the temptation.

BRACED for trouble, always under strain, the Israelis have to cope not only with their enemies but with difficult friends. In mid-December, Jerusalemites were asking, "Have you read the Alsop letter? Have you ever seen anything like it? This must be Kissinger's work. Isn't it incredible?" They were speaking of an article by Joseph Alsop in *The New York Times Magazine* of December 14, 1975, called "Open Letter to an Israeli Friend." The "Dear Amos" to whom this letter was addressed is Amos Eiran, director general of the Office of the Prime Minister and also the Prime Minister's political adviser. Eiran, formerly counselor of the Israeli Embassy in Washington, is in his forties—a firm-looking, attractive man. The symmetry of his features makes him look more calm than would be possible for anyone in his position. He has the same deliberate, unexcited manner as his chief, Rabin.

I quickly obtain a copy of the Alsop letter. My first reaction is that a personal letter is sent directly to one's friend, not published in the papers. Alsop has recently announced his retirement, but a world-famous journalist can't be expected to put aside his interest in public questions, renounce his magic like Shakespeare's Prospero, break his staff, and drown his book. Prospero had only one small island to give up, not the global interests of a superpower. The "Dear Amos" letter reveals that Alsop has not turned from politics to prayer and that his state of mind is as imperial as it ever was. He speaks of himself modestly enough. He is merely Mr. Eiran's Ameri-

can friend. "Any American must always put American
interests first, so I've thought a lot about the way Israel
affects American interests. Some of the effects have been
adverse, rather obviously, as in the area of American
relations with the Arab world. Yet such considerations
are heavily outweighed, in my opinion, as soon as you
apply the acid test to the Israel-American relationship.
It is a macabre test. Because of Israel's perilous national
situation, we Americans always have to think about how
America would be affected by Israel's actual destruction." Alsop is a great friend of Israel. He was not one
from the beginning. Mr. Rabin has told me in conversation that Alsop was not altogether in favor of a Jewish
state in Palestine but that he many years ago changed his
mind. He is full of admiration for the military virtues of
the Israelis. He has supported Israel through many
crises. Although he speaks bluntly to "Dear Amos"
about the destruction of Israel, he adds, "Which heaven
forfend!" He goes on to say that if this were to come to
pass, "such a flood of guilt and hatred and recrimination"
would result "as might fatally corrode the whole fabric
of our society. Hence I have long believed that we Americans must assure Israel's survival, if only to assure the
survival of those American values that I cherish most.
There you have my personal bottom line where your
country is concerned."

Why is it that Alsop is writing such a letter, warning
Israel that it stands in danger of destruction and remind-
ing it that it has only one protector? It is because "bad
trouble has begun between Israel and America." For one
thing, Alsop is shocked by Israel's ingratitude to Secretary of State Kissinger. By working out an agreement
with Egypt in the Sinai Desert, Kissinger obtained a
desperately needed breathing space for Israel. Yet everywhere in Israel last spring Alsop found evidence of "an
anti-Kissinger campaign." One high personage told
Alsop, "We'd be better off without a Jew at the State Department." Even "so great a woman as Golda Meir,"
whom Kissinger "truly reveres," allowed herself to make

a crack about "my lost friend, Henry."

A hostile Congress grudgingly ratified Kissinger's Sinai bargain, Alsop continues. Israel can by no means take for granted the continued support of American public opinion. Opinion is turning against it, and ways must be found to reverse the changing trend. And what is the cause of this dangerous shift in attitude? It dates from the so-called March 1975 "crisis." Kissinger would not have resumed his shuttle diplomacy between Jerusalem and Cairo if he hadn't been invited by both Egypt and Israel to go on trying. And "he would have refused to set foot on Air Force One last March if he had not believed that after suitable haggling, the Israeli Government would finally meet President Sadat's rock-bottom requirements for an interim agreement." Prime Minister Rabin, says Alsop, had indicated that "he was confident of carrying his government with him." He had "unintentionally misled" the secretary of state. This was why President Ford was moved to send an angry personal letter to Mr. Rabin. In a word, probably without intending to deceive, Israel had behaved deceitfully. There was intrigue in the Israeli Cabinet. A putative rival of Rabin's, ambitious to replace him, was in a position to know that Israel's general staff held a withdrawal from the Mitla and Gidi passes to be militarily acceptable. This rival declared that Rabin could not accept such a concession. Alsop says, "I have a horror of the bad American practice of choosing up sides in other people's politics, so I shall identify this member of the Rabin Cabinet no further, except that it is necessary to add that he personally controlled eight votes in the Knesset."

A certain disciple betrayed Jesus. It would be improper for an outsider to mention names, but he did it with a kiss, and his initials were J.I.

Negotiations with Egypt and Israel then stopped, and Kissinger, though perfectly understanding Rabin's difficulties, was disappointed. President Ford, however, was sufficiently vexed to fire off a letter. Alsop may have a horror of the bad American practice of choosing up sides in other people's politics, but this does not prevent his telling Mr. Eiran, "On an issue of war or peace of the utmost importance to your American partners, Israel's viciously competitive domestic politics had been allowed to take command. That, and only that, was what really started the trouble between your country and mine—at least on the American side, which is the side that endangers you. Unfairly enough, of course, trouble with America can be fatal to Israel, but trouble with Israel does not gravely endanger the U.S."

It would be difficult for a political observer—and in Israel every citizen is a political observer—to know what construction to put on this. Alsop was saying, bluntly enough, get your house in order, shape up, don't step out of line. Were these threats inspired by the secretary of state? By the President? Or had Alsop taken it upon himself, a private American citizen but also by his bearing a man of destiny, to crack destiny's whip in the finest Toulouse-Lautrec circus style?

Israel, Alsop says, has not adjusted itself to the fact that America's relations with the Arab countries have changed. "Such an adjustment is now more urgent than ever, unless you Israelis want still worse trouble between our two countries. Making the adjustment by no means requires you to bow invariably to American views. There will always be room for serious discussion. But the new situation [in which America draws first Egypt and then the rest of the Arab world away from Russian influence] most certainly requires you to keep Israeli domestic politics strictly out of all future Middle Eastern negotiations vitally involving American national policy. And I must regretfully add that it further requires you to avoid any future attempts to influence our national policy in the Middle East by interfering in American domestic politics. Unhappily, this was precisely what you did last spring after the negotiations broke down in March." Alsop speaks only of Israel's failure to "adjust"; he says nothing about Egyptian recognition of Israel's right to existence. Nor does he mention Arab efforts to influence American policy in the Middle East. Is there no boycott of companies that do business with Israel? Are there no Arab lobbyists registered?

People in Jerusalem asked me what I thought of all this. Had Kissinger put Alsop up to writing such a letter? I answered that I was no sort of specialist and that such Byzantine intrigue was beyond me. Kissinger had—I was about to say that he had many detractors in Israel, but what is more like the truth is that he has few admirers. Neither he nor the Israelis know quite what to make of the fact that he is a Jew. The Israelis might complain of him less if he were a Southern Baptist or an Irish Catholic. He is widely believed to have delayed sending help during the Yom Kippur War because he wanted the Egyptians to enjoy a limited victory and recover self-esteem. In the end, so goes the story, it was Defense Secretary James R. Schlesinger who went to Nixon and pressed him to fly supplies immediately to Israel. In Matti Golan's *The Secret Conversations of Henry Kissinger,* published in 1976, the secretary of state is accused of duplicity in negotiating a cease-fire agreement with the Russians that prevented the Israelis from destroying the two Egyptian armies they had trapped. It seems that before taking off for Moscow at the most critical moment of the Yom Kippur War Kissinger had promised Israel's Ambassador Simcha Dinitz he would go slowly in his talks with the Russians in order to give Israel time to achieve its military objectives, but according to Mr. Golan he had no sooner landed than the cease-fire terms were agreed upon and President Nixon at once asked Golda Meir to announce her acceptance of the deal Kissinger had made without consultation. Mrs. Meir was "shocked and furious." During a Cabinet meeting she received a message from the British foreign minister urging her to agree to the cease-fire. "She and the other ministers now realized that not only did Kissinger not consult her, but he informed her of the agreement after he told the British foreign minister." Israel felt that it had been insulted—even betrayed (by Kissinger). Possibly the Russians threatened intervention. That they would have let Israel destroy two Egyptian armies and perhaps even take Cairo is unlikely. What, in any case, would Israel have done with Cairo? Another week's fighting would have cost a thousand more Israeli lives, as Abba Eban sensibly said during our lunch at the Knesset. What in Kissinger is called "betrayal" might, in a non-Jewish secretary of state, be accepted with a shrug as diplomacy—one of the normal forms of perfidy, that is.

Alsop is an agreeable person to meet. The expression of his rather narrow New England face suggests that he has got rid of much that is superfluous, that he has seen all the grandeur and the squalor of the century and that he has qualified himself to enter deeper realms of thought than most people have the opportunity to enter. He looks as though he had undergone the Anglo-Saxon ordeal, suffered all the privations, accepted all the responsibilities. Very much the New England aristocrat, but worldly, tough, obstinate: he never ceases to emit the sense that he is a man of destiny—American style, I would add. I once spent an afternoon with him in Georgetown. He told me stirring stories of his experiences in China. I remember also one of his anecdotes about a lady at the court of Queen Anne—or perhaps at Versailles—who washed her hair so seldom that on one occasion a family of mice was found nesting in her coiffure. He told me also a rather good joke about a southern senator in a Washington brothel—in the good old sleepy days when senators had time to go to brothels. He talked eighteenth-century furniture, Chinese antiques, Greek archaeology, literature. He might or might not have known what he was talking about; I was having too good a time to care. He went from high culture to GI slang with no trouble at all. And he was, distinctly, no mere syndicated columnist. He took a large view of the fate of nations, of the plane-tary struggle of good and evil, of the role America was playing in the twentieth century, and of his own partici-pation in historical events. You were to come away after such an afternoon feeling that he wore his power lightly, but that there was a lot of it and it could be used with devastating effect. But how these men of destiny do pick on people! The "Dear Amos" letter speaks of "flagrant foreign interference" and "planned intervention" by Israel in American affairs, making trouble for Kissinger in Congress, "arm-twisting" by friends of Israel—and such friends can be none other than American Jews. Here Alsop sounds a little like General George Brown of the Joint Chiefs and Ernest Bevin during his worst seizures of anti-Zionism. (Ben-Gurion was always careful to distinguish between anti-Semitism and anti-Zionism; he did not believe that Bevin was anti-Semitic.)

The fact that Israel is dependent on the United States is plain enough. What is it that tempts an American publicist to make what everyone can see so cruelly explicit?

FROM a narrow window at the Van Leer Foundation I watch foreign dignitaries arriving next door, at the President's residence. There is a guard of honor, and the band plays "Hatikvah"—not the most cheerful of national anthems. The limousines come and go, smooth and somber, and the motorcycles, buzzing and rattling. I treat myself to a stroll in the New—or newer—City and visit Herbert Stein's bookshop. Mr. Stein is a fine old-fashioned dealer—lean, pale, furrowed, wearing a large light-brown mustache. Unsorted at the rear of his shop are moldering heaps of books in German, Arabic, French, English, and Hebrew. Mr. Stein has little to offer the paperback-buying tourist. He is strong on historians, sages, mystics, and Talmudic commentators, and on German novels of the twenties beautifully printed on the sort of paper one doesn't see any more. Also travel books, guide books, cookery books, and the best sellers of my youth: Vicki Baum, George Warwick Deeping, Emil Ludwig—Richard Harding Davis, even.

Later in the day my friend Professor Joseph Ben-David takes me to the swelling Souk, the public market. On Fridays it closes early. We watch the last-minute pre-Sabbath rush. Perishables are cheap as zero hour approaches. We buy bananas and roses and tiny mandarins no bigger than walnuts. Ben-David has brought along a net bag to hold our purchases. Not a mile away from the commercial center of Jerusalem, but the Oriental and North African merchants and hucksters make it seem more distant. Boys push barrows, shouting

"Hello! Hello!" to clear the path. As the stalls are closing, muffled beggar women come to pick through the refuse. The air is not clear this afternoon; it is gray, warm, and heavy. We lock the flowers and fruit in Ben-David's car and walk in the small streets. Those with cisterns underneath swell slightly in the middle, moundlike. A few adolescents are kicking their footballs in miniature playgrounds. In all communities—Kurdish, Yemenite, Yiddish-speaking Polish—everyone else is washing, sweeping, dressing, and preening for the Sabbath. Older men in their fur hats and long coats are already pacing slowly and with a special air toward their synagogues. All this will go, says Ben-David, as central Jerusalem expands. He knows these tiny communities well. Nearly thirty years ago he was a social worker in the neighborhood, rehabilitating young delinquents. I have learned to think twice before offering Ben-David an opinion on any matter, because his tolerance for vague views and inexact formulations is limited. He is a short, compact man. His blue gaze is mild enough, and he can even look contemplative and dreamy, but he fires up easily. Our discussions would turn into arguments if I didn't give ground, so, because I respect him, I invariably back off. Besides, I come from Chicago and will return to Chicago; this makes me much less contentious. Still, because he looks so mild, when we meet and he smiles and holds his hand out gently, I always note the hardness of his palm and the strength of his grip.

We go into a Yemenite synagogue. The early arrivals have left their shoes at the door, Arab style. Bearded, dark-faced, they sit along the wall. You see their stockinged feet on the footrests of their lecterns. It is traditional on Friday afternoons to read the Song of Songs aloud, and they are reciting or chanting it now, in long lines, un-European in intonation. This chanting resembles the collective recitations you hear when passing Arab schoolrooms.

Ben-David knows a lot about the lives of Jews from the Arab countries. He often makes the point that they, too, are refugees who fled from persecution and whose property was confiscated. World opinion concentrates on the Palestinian refugees while these Oriental Jews—nearly a million of them—are given no consideration. It is inevitable that he and I should turn to politics. Sightseeing is all very well, but our heads are full of news, omens, and speculations.

Ben-David, who closely follows the American press, says, "Congress seems to me to have gone wild on the Angolan question. It has cut across the President's power to act in foreign affairs. By refusing publicly to support him it has notified the Russians that they can do as they like. It goes over the head of the executive. It's nothing but appeasement, isn't it? The United States has no foreign policy any more. It no longer behaves like a great power. Washington has let go the controls." What he is saying comes to this: Israel is dependent upon America for its very survival, and American foreign policy is in retreat. The agonized attention of Israelis is fixed upon developments in the United States. Such concentrated attention comes close to being a sort of magical activity to avert a disaster. From the Congress Ben-David moves to Henry Kissinger: "The Russians have used his détente to change the balance of power in the world in their favor. He has no real policy." And, "What sort of person can he be? I think his personal taste is for the jet set. He is one of the beautiful people, as you call them."

We look into a few more synagogues, but I am no longer in a Sabbath mood. Ben-David has a genuine feeling for the quarter and for the peace of the Sabbath, but he is evidently thinking of other things—of Russians and Arabs and petro-dollars, of European indifference and American disorder and mindlessness. I go home to Alexandra and give her the roses. They are dark red, almost a black-crimson color. She is very pleased with them.

S UDDENLY I who never knew a thing about battle-ships, aircraft carriers and submarines find myself boning up on the Sixth Fleet and Russian naval power in the Mediterranean. The Americans continue to keep some sort of hold on the northern littoral, says one of my experts, but they are losing out in Portugal, are slipping in Spain, may not be safe for long in Italy, and are becoming shaky in Greece. Suddenly for several days my head is filled with statistics of "ship-days of operation" and I am injected with the dread names of weapons. Since 1967 the Russians have deployed between forty and a hundred ships in the Mediterranean, including light cruisers of the *Kresta* and the *Kynda* classes. One of their two helicopter carriers, the *Moskva* or the *Leningrad,* is always on Mediterranean assignment. In the autumn of 1975 the new forty-thousand-ton carrier *Kiev* was due to emerge from the Black Sea. Under these siren waters, there are about a dozen Russian submarines. There are land-based Russian planes that can attack the Sixth Fleet and return without refueling—the Soviet Badger force. The Americans, on the other hand, have the superior F-14. The F-14 "can stand off at some distance from the carrier force, and with the Phoenix missile can acquire and destroy six targets simultaneously without engaging any target at close range," explains Dr. Alvin Cottrell.* He adds, "It would still

---

*"Issues in the Mediterranean," The Chicago Council on Foreign Relations, 1975, p. 28.

require an estimated 7 to 10 years before the Soviets
would be able to operate effectively an American-type
aircraft carrier with steam catapults and the most modern fighters such as the F-4 and the F-14. The U.S. Navy
has a long history of operating these ships, and it is an
experience that has been passed from one generation
to another." And yet there are the new boys, inexperi-
enced but bristling with frightful armaments. They have
never used them in earnest. No one knows how effective
their green crews are and whether their officers are any
good—I take this in breathlessly. To think that only yes-
terday I was reading Henry James and Baudelaire's
journals. Today my thoughts are all on the Soviet
surveillance satellites sparkling in the night skies, and
the control of what professionals call the "choke points":
the Strait of Gibraltar, Sicily, the area near the western
entrance to Piraeus. The Russians have deftly used the
Cyprus dispute, the differences among the Arab states,
even the troubles between Spain and England over
Gibraltar to isolate the United States and weaken its
position in the Mediterranean. Israel is its only dependable ally there. Western monopoly of the Mediterranean
is at an end. The Russians have established themselves
as the dominant power. In the words of Dr. Cottrell,
"They would not be overly optimistic if they believed
themselves on the threshold of reaching . . . paramountcy
in the area." They might easily have landed troops in
Egypt in 1973. And if the Lebanese government were to
ask the United States for military help in its struggle to
survive, the Americans might have to answer that Soviet
naval power makes this impossible.

POSTHUMOUSLY published, the three-volume study *The Venture of Islam,* by my late colleague at the University of Chicago Marshall Hodgson, is being favorably reviewed by scholars. Now that the reading fit is on me again, I intend to buy the three new volumes. Marshall was a vegetarian, a pacifist, and a Quaker—most odd, most unhappy, a quirky charmer. He was pleasantly contradictory in his view of the world— why should a pacifist fall in love with militant Islam? Marshall's small daughters, the twins, had a congenital disease of the nervous system, which eventually proved fatal. Often I met Marshall on the fifth floor of the Social Science Building—he refused to use the elevator, he ran up the stairs—and we talked. The painful subject was never avoided. I asked how the children were. They didn't sleep well. He and his wife were up with them in the night, spelling each other. So his sleepless face was often swollen, congested; his eyes bulged; and he was hoarse, almost incomprehensible, because he had been reading fairy tales to the girls. He said, nearly voiceless, how heartbreaking it was, how much the children understood. They seemed to realize that they would die. Then with tears in his eyes he hurried back to his studies. I went to his house now and then. The Hodgsons lived in graduate-student-slum style in an apartment building in Hyde Park, not far from Jimmy's famous tavern, that cheerful center of good will and caked dirt. At the Hodgsons' you ate vanilla ice cream and discussed serious subjects. The children's heads were always bowed; perhaps their necks were weak. The family were "thee"-using Quakers. Marshall, soaked in his subject, thoroughly pedantic, had no informal manner. He was always and everywhere the same—earnest, theoretical, high-minded, stubbornly virtuous. He kept himself physically fit. He ate his esculents and succulents with an avid red mouth in small quick bites. At a Committee on Social Thought dinner, while holding a big strawberry with the fingers of both hands, squirrel style, he looked sidelong down into my plate with its steak and asked, "Is your carrion well cooked?"

He was romantic about Islam. He told me, and probably was right, that I didn't *understand.* Though he once wrote me a letter saying that he wanted to join the Mississippi civil-rights marchers, he had no sympathy whatever with Zionism. After the war of 1967 he cried out, "You have no business in Arab lands, you Jews!" In the heat of argument he then said many rash things. Of course few people do understand the complexities of Arab history, and it made Marshall frantic when he saw a pattern of Western political ideas being imposed ignorantly on the Middle East. But he knew as little about Jews as I did about Arabs. Nation-states have seldom if ever been created without violence and injustice. Hodgson believed that the Jews had behaved as though the Arabs were an inferior, colonial sort of people and not the heirs of a great civilization. Of course the Arabs had themselves come as conquerors, many centuries ago. But one didn't present such arguments to Marshall. The Arabs were his people. *He* failed to understand what Israel meant to the Jews. It wasn't that the Jews didn't matter—he was a Quaker and a liberal, a man of humane sentiments—but that he didn't know quite how they mattered.

Some years ago, Hodgson went out to jog on a boiling Chicago afternoon and died of heart failure.

WHEREVER you go in Israel you are subject to recognitions. You see familiar eyes, noses, complexions, postures, gestures. Professor Harkabi and my Cousin Louie, of Lachine, are much alike. Or, to take another pair: is this bald, deep-voiced, big-chested man the manager of a factory in Nazareth or is he the son of Dr. Tir, who became a captain in the U.S. Merchant Marine? You begin to suspect that a diverse band of spirits is operating out of a limited number of bodily and facial types. The experience is both pleasant and unpleasant. The eyes, freckles, mouths, fingers are utterly familiar, but these resemblances are misleading. When you meet party leaders and Cabinet ministers who look like Montreal insurance agents or Brooklyn high-school teachers, you begin to be disconcerted. For you think of chiefs of state as distinctly different. They are remote, like Woodrow Wilson; they blink nobly over the heads of the multitude, like FDR; they are filled with a peculiar historical essence, like General de Gaulle.

True, Ben-Gurion looked like a leader. Golda Meir, when I met her in 1959, was fussing over her grandchildren, but even on that occasion she had the look of a central personality. Prime Minister Rabin has no such look, though he may acquire it if he remains long enough in office. Why have political leaders stopped putting themselves into their faces in the classical style? John F. Kennedy certainly had a look, but Lyndon Johnson seemed to assert that he needed no look—he was *it*.

As for Richard Nixon, looking does not figure in his imagination; his gaze is something from which he apparently withdraws into the depths where the real action is. And I think of other political leaders I've seen—of Willy Brandt putting on a gift Stetson hat beside a trout stream in Colorado, of Harold Wilson's untidy hair and his unthrilling handshake. The French, I suppose, will be the last to give up the charged look. It was stirring to meet St.-John Perse, the diplomat and poet. He widened his eyes shamanistically as he pronounced your name, he behaved like a clairvoyant, his gaze pierced your mask dramatically. His was a constantly coiling and uncoiling presence. But even the French are beginning to look like everyone else. One Israeli leader described Valéry Giscard d'Estaing to me as a computerized personality: "He is a technocrat, and he looks it." Leonid Brezhnev is supposed to be concerned about his appearance. He is said to have asked an American diplomat, "Do you think I have a brutal face?" This is the sort of thing you hear when you leave your desk and enter life.

Prime Minister Rabin's quality is of the plainer sort. The Rabin Alexandra and I meet at lunch looks like a private person in a difficult public position. A strongly built man of middle height, he has a powerful neck, his face is enlarged by a retreating hairline, his complexion is light, reddish. He seems intelligent, brave, and up against it. It is obvious that he is straining continually to make sense; to accept such an obligation doesn't make life simpler. He speaks English correctly, with many Israeli gutturals. He may not have a charged look, but the charge is there. You feel it also in his house, although the Rabin residence is not imposing. If it weren't for the men with machine guns at the door, you would think yourself in a comfortable house in Washington or Philadelphia. We drink sherry with the Rabins and Mr. and Mrs. Amos Eiran. Amos Eiran is Director General of the Office of the Prime Minister. Then we are joined at lunch by young Rabin, a soldier home on leave, and his girl friend. The young people do not speak during the meal.

The Prime Minister's wife is slender and dark, and a spirited talker. ("She has class," Alexandra says later.) Mrs. Rabin knows, however, that we have come to hear what her husband has to say.

But what does the leader of a most troubled country tell his American guests? You can be sure that he will do no more than repeat what he has often said in public. What else can he do? I am not a journalist. I am another, dreamier sort of creature. Just the same, Mr. Rabin must be careful with me.

For my part, I have a horror of wasting the time of people who are busy and burdened. I recall an anecdote about Lyndon Johnson: to an interviewer whom he had intimidated and who was fluttering and fumbling, the President is supposed to have said, "What kind of chicken-shit question is *that* to ask the head of the most powerful nation in the world?" How well I can understand the unwillingness of Samuel Johnson to bandy civilities with his sovereign.

But Mr. Rabin did not make me feel that I was wasting his time. He said at lunch what he was able to say. But I wasn't here to make a scoop. I was here to observe, to sense a condition or absorb qualities. I think that Mr. Rabin knew this; Mrs. Rabin clearly understood it and tried to guide the conversation helpfully. Rabin's manner is deliberate and measured. A man in his position is obliged to appear stable—"normal." But there is nothing at all "normal" in his situation. His government is shaky, he has to cope with domestic infighting, with the strength of the Arabs and their petro-dollars, with Russian pressure, and with Washington. Congress is, for the moment, pro-Israel, but the State Department is not. The report of Harold Saunders, deputy assistant secretary for Near Eastern and South Asian affairs, to the House Committee on International Relations stressing the importance of the Palestinian question dismayed the Israelis; they took it as evidence that the pro-Arab faction in the State Department was being encouraged for tactical reasons by Mr. Kissinger himself. Here, then, is Mr. Rabin holding on to stability in the midst of violent tremors. The situation is desperately complicated. No wonder that his color is high.

We begin with a light subject. Since Amos himself is here, it is inevitable that we should talk of Alsop and his "Dear Amos" letter. Although Alsop speaks of the destruction of Israel, he needn't be taken too seriously; he isn't, in himself, dangerous. He is in some sense the friend he claims to be, and he is certainly diverting. According to Rabin, Alsop became a supporter of the Jewish state after he had gone into the field with Israeli soldiers. Having roughed it for several days with fighting men, he returned full of enthusiasm for these Jews, so different from any he had ever known. I observe that Alsop is concerned about the decline of American standards. I think he takes it hard that the Protestant Majority is no longer culturally and intellectually dominant. Rabin, who came to know Alsop well when he served as ambassador in Washington, says that they had often discussed the subject and agrees that Alsop feels it keenly. Alsop is a violent attitudinizer, and one of the attitudes he strikes is that of the patrician American, a vanishing breed. When Alsop scolds Israel and American Jewry, he is perhaps expressing his unhappiness over the waning influence of his class.

We turn to other matters. The Arabs, says Rabin, are not interested in territorial concessions and will never be satisfied with them. They consider themselves owners and masters of this land. Jews and Christians are tolerated in Muslim society only as second-class citizens. There is therefore no point in making offers, saying to the Arabs we will give you this or that piece of ground in return for recognition and peace. The hope is that as the Arab countries grow rich and modernize themselves they will grow less hostile, more concerned to produce goods than to fight. I say nothing, but I doubt it greatly. You can test Rabin's theory by looking to Lebanon, where up-to-date fanatical extremists are at this moment killing people in the streets of once prosperous Beirut. Feudal monarchs are probably easier to deal with than the European-influenced young left-wing future leaders. Rabin says next that the Arabs' strength will shrink as Europe and America develop independent energy resources. How long will that take, I ask myself. Six years? Eight? Ten? And during that time Israel must continue to get billions of dollars from the United States, which has its own interests in the Arab world to think about. I don't say this to Mr. Rabin, either. I have come to listen, not to differ. So I merely remark that the United States isn't solving its energy problems very quickly.

I ask Mr. Rabin just how he would describe the Russian aims in this region. He says that the Russians produce disorder in the Middle East for the discomfiture of the United States, but that they will avoid a world war. Direct confrontations are unnecessary. The Russians can succeed better by indirection. They hope to Finlandize Western Europe. When Tito dies, they will try to move into Yugoslavia. They do not welcome the new democratic line of the Italian and French Communist parties, but if those parties should take over, America might draw away from Western Europe, leaving Russia as the sole Continental power. Hence Finlandization. This term, now widely used, signifies that some of Russia's conquests can get the soft treatment. The Soviets have not done in Helsinki what they have done in Prague.

Toward the end of the meal, the talk turns to an important and neglected subject: public opinion. Rabin admits that Israel has not been effective in its publicity. I say that Arab propaganda has become extremely effective and that the Arabs have succeeded in winning worldwide public support. Yes, they have a talent for that sort of thing, Mr. Rabin says; he implies that this is not one of Israel's major problems. I disagree.

The Arabs enjoy a significant advantage in the sympathy of the left. Raymond Aron once estimated that the French intelligentsia was "80% Marxianised." The French intelligentsia has remained immensely prestigious—immensely and inexplicably, because there are

intellectuals in the United States who would tell you that
Paris today is culturally on a level with Buenos Aires.
But the prestige of centuries is not exhausted in a few
decades and French attitudes matter greatly in many
parts of the world. In France, Germany, England, and
the United States, leftist intellectuals, when they discuss
Israel, continue to use the Marxist-Leninist categories:
finance capital, colonialism, and imperialism. Arab nationalists have only to call out the anti-capitalist, anti-
imperialist slogans to gain support in the West. There is,
besides, a considerable tradition of left-wing anti-Semitism in France and Germany. The history of Socialist
anti-Semitism is, alas, long and dirty, but I doubt that
much of this older, leftist anti-Semitism has survived
among European intellectuals. They are not overtly anti-
Semitic. It is enough for them that Israel, living on
American subsidies, is serving America's imperialist
aims in the Middle East. (Sartre, by the way, has denied
this.) But there is in Europe a full reservoir of left-wing
sympathies that Egypt, Syria, and the PLO can and do
tap. Many American radicals share these sympathies.

I briefly try to persuade Rabin that Israel had better
give some thought to the media intelligentsia in the
United States. I say that the country is in a let's-clean-it-
up mood. We've cleaned up Vietnam, cleaned up Water-
gate, we are now cleaning up the CIA and the FBI and
the Medicaid frauds. If the media were to lay the problem of the Palestinians or peace in the Middle East before American public opinion while the country is in this
impatient state, calling on the government to "clean it
up," it might be disastrous for Israel. Rabin says he is
aware of all this. I doubt that Israel's highest officials
understand the danger. I judge by what I have seen and
heard at home. At home the basic facts are not widely
known. Very few Americans seem to know, for instance,
that when the U.N., in 1947, proposed the creation of
two separate states, Jewish and Arab, the Jews accepted
the provision for the political independence of the Palestinian Arabs. It was the Arab nations which rejected the

U.N. plan, vowing to resist partition by force and assaulting the Jewish community in Palestine. The Arabs have succeeded in persuading American public opinion that the Jews descended upon Palestine after World War II and evicted the native population with arms.

Professor Bernard Lewis, of Princeton, takes the view that Israel must win its struggle in the United States and it must have the support of American public opinion. He is obviously right. Already, "evenhanded" (i.e., unfriendly) journalistic strategists are reconsidering the military importance of Israel. To "reconsider" in this manner is to suggest (evenhandedly) that Israel is not indispensable to American interests. From this it follows that it might be better to buy in with the Arab world. Raymond Aron puts it simply in *The Imperial Republic: The United States and the World: 1945–1973*: the United States has become Israel's protector and ally. "Is this alignment attributable to the influence of the Jewish community in America? Partly, without the slightest doubt; decisions on the external actions of the American republic are always subject to pressures. . . . Where the Middle East and Israel are concerned, the representatives of the American Jewish Committee lobby the Secretary of State, as do the representatives of the big oil companies. In the case in point the latter have not prevailed." He was writing in 1974. But how long will this state of affairs continue? In one of those "objective," half-menacing conversations that leave me with a sick headache, an American expert with State Department connections said to me apropos of the warnings in Alsop's "Dear Amos" letter: "What if the President were to become irritated or angry with Jewish lobbyists? And suppose he were to burst out and say publicly, in a press conference, that the Jewish lobby was exerting too much pressure? What would the effect of such a statement be? If a President so much as hinted it, it would make bad trouble. Of course the American political system would itself then be in bad trouble. But Israel should not count on the power of the American Jewish lobby. It should consider, too, the long-range effects of the lobbying."

As soon as Alsop speaks of the "arm-twisting" tactics used by American friends of Israel, the shadows of dual loyalty and of second-class citizenship begin to move in quickly from the horizon. Such shadows swept over France in 1967 when de Gaulle, in his historic press conference, characterized the Jews as a people "sure of itself and domineering." By so doing, he gave pain to French Jews—he probably frightened and shocked some of them. Of course he spoke as a "monarch," displeased by the disobedience of the Israelis who went to war against his wishes in June.

WE are invited to dinner by some of Alexandra's friends—like her, teaching mathematics at the Hebrew University. Pleasant people. The children, a boy and a girl, are delightful. They come up to the table and examine us boldly, pacing around the room like small lions. They look into our plates to see how foreigners eat cutlets. We are curious creatures, and we make them laugh.

The conversation, as usual, quickly becomes serious. You do not hear much small talk in Jerusalem. Inflation, high taxes, the austerity program make moonlighting necessary. We are told that many wives are going back to work. Alexandra has noticed how busy mathematical colleagues have become. They have to do more teaching; they have less time for research.

After dinner two more guests arrive, Dr. and Mrs. Eliahu Rips. Rips comes from Riga. When the Russians went into Czechoslovakia, Rips, a mathematics student, set himself on fire in protest. The flames were beaten out and Rips was sent to an insane asylum. While there, without books, he solved a famous problem in algebra. When he was released, he emigrated and reached Israel not long before the Yom Kippur War. Since he had no army training, he went to a gas station and offered to work for nothing, feeling that he must make a contribution to Israel's defense. So for some months he pumped gas, unpaid. He is now teaching at the Hebrew University. He has become not only Orthodox but very devout. Four days a week he studies the Talmud in a yeshiva. Devout

Talmudic mathematicians, physicists, biologists are not rare in Israel. At all hours, the houses of study in Jerusalem are full.

Rips has recently married a young woman, French by birth and punctiliously Orthodox. Being French and Orthodox, she is elegantly observant. She has her head not merely covered as the law prescribes, but beautifully done up in a silk scarf. She has the look of one of those dark Rebeccas with whom the Crusaders fell in love. She not only binds her head up elegantly, but is elegantly talkative. Our subject: science and religion; the boundaries of scientific knowledge, the certainty that there are other kinds of knowing. Rips himself, the algebraic genius, contributes little to the conversation, though he follows it closely. He is a slender, clear-skinned, good-looking young man. The first thing you observe is the quiet manner of his sitting. A whole philosophy is in it. His legs are easy, his wrists and hands are easy. In a madhouse, all he required was a chair to sit in. I remember during the conversation something I once heard about Leibniz— that he could sit reflecting for three days. When I see Rips sitting, I begin to understand how, doing the calculations in his head, he might find the answer to an unsolved problem. What is unimaginable is that this gently abstracted young man should be capable of dousing himself with gasoline and setting himself afire.

WHETHER people who are greatly respected know what they are saying: Laura (Riding) Jackson warns of the danger that "thinkers" can constitute for the rest of humanity. She sees this danger in the linguistic forms in which their thought is cast. These can "capture minds hypnotically by the force of the personal will infused into them." Another way of describing this is to call it, as she does, "a political style of intellectual performance." She goes on to speak of the "tradition of an intellectual-leader race of masterminds."* No one who wanted to compile a list of these masterminds now living could omit the name of Sartre. I can't say I agree that the problem is one of linguistic forms, but I respond to her suggestion that in every generation we recognize a leader race of masterminds whose ideas ("class-struggle," "Oedipus complex," "identity crisis") come down over us like butterfly nets.

Reading Sartre on the Middle East, I wonder whether he really knows what he is saying. And yet he is an eminent writer, a *normalien*, and people I respect esteem him. I remember talking about him with Edmund Wilson. Wilson was enthusiastic about him. Why? Perhaps because they were both against many of the same things. Wilson said that Sartre was indeed vulnerable to many kinds of criticism, but that he was, after all, a man of letters. It sounds even more significant in French—an *homme de lettres*, one of that wonderful band, the Voltaires, the

---

*"Bertrand Russell and Others: The Idea of the Master-Mind," *Antaeus* 21/22, pp. 125–135.

Diderots, the Renans, the Sainte-Beuves, Taines, and Valérys. No generation without its *hommes de lettres* could call itself properly civilized. So a Sartre is a valuable item in civilization's inventory. Raymond Aron, a man very different from Wilson, says that, in arguments with Sartre, "I was often quite definitely right. Even then, however, I realized that his was the creative spirit." Social scientists, making no creative claim themselves, sometimes carelessly put the creative spirit into the first hand they see extended.

In the late forties, I used to go down to the Pont Royal bar to look at Sartre; I can't say he looked at me. Americans were not popular with him. Matters were different sixty years ago. When John Dos Passos and E. E. Cummings came to France, it was to drive ambulances in the Great War and they were warmly greeted, or thought they were. Eager young Americans who hurried to Paris after World War II got icy treatment. But then I think of someone like Kafū Nagai, a writer of genius who read Maupassant and other French novelists in Tokyo early in the 1890s, and, falling in love with them, set out to see them. It took Kafū a long time to cross the American Continent. He stopped in Chicago. He spent more than a year at Ypsilanti State Teacher's College, in Michigan. When at last he reached Paris, he could find no French writers who would talk to him. Those of us who arrived from America in the late forties were not the first to experience pangs of unrequited love.

I had read *La Nausée* and liked it, but only as a curiosity—it didn't touch me in any vital place. The *Chemins de la Liberté*, with its moving-picture methods, its *simultanéité*, I found too self-consciously historical, too frantic and overheated. Wyndham Lewis came up with the right term for it. He called it "cyclone literature." Only plagues, wars, massacres, crisis situations could, in Sartre's view, reveal the essential, the total human being: "*l'homme tout entier.*"

The *homme tout entier* must be driven from the thickets of philistinism, where he likes to find cover. Our

ancestors built houses, created our culture, gave us their
great men, practiced modest virtues, and confined themselves to temperate regions, says Wyndham Lewis, inter-
preting Sartre in 1952 in *The Writer and the Absolute*.
Whereas we, familiar with world wars, holocausts,
bombardments, *coups d'état*, "we are necessarily of a
heroic mould. Our virtues are either terrific, or else we
are submen of the vilest kind. These immediate ancestors
of ours, of comfortable prosperous periods, before 'air-
power' held forth the promise to dash you to pieces or
shrivel you up from the sky, or the revolutionary brought
back the thrilling atmosphere of the Inquisition or the
auto da fé, are to be pitied (and, however we may protest, looked down upon) for never having had the opportunity to be 'metaphysical' or to have felt 'the pressure of
history.' " This history is wide-screen or Cinerama history, and we are seated in the first row watching the
brutal stampede in natural color and *tout nu*.

Baudelaire, very different from Sartre in that he had
less formal education and came at things with a mini-
mum of theoretical apparatus, speaks of his wild excitement during the Revolution of 1848. And what was the
cause of that excitement? "The desire for revenge," he
explains simply in "Mon Coeur Mis à Nu," "natural
pleasure in destruction." From this he somewhat disasso-
ciates himself, for what is natural is to him suspect. Elsewhere in his journals, Baudelaire refers to an "aristocratic pleasure" in giving offense. It was to the bourgeois,
of course, that offense was at that time given. And now I
sometimes think that in the twentieth century it is America which has been chosen by history to replace the bourgeois, while France as a nation has been elevated to the
aristocratic position. The United States is in a certain
sense the chosen object of its aristocratic snooting.

Between Sartre and any given problem in politics there
has always stood the United States. There are in the
world two superpowers, but only one has seemed to him
positively evil. When he discussed the Middle East, his
first concern as a friend of Israel was to dissociate Israel

from American interests. In an interview I have been reading, written in 1969,* Sartre expresses great sympathy with Israel, says that in the Israeli-Arab conflict there is no total justice on one side or the other, and he defends Israel against the charge that it is the instrument of American imperialism. What is more important, Sartre explains, is that "the Israeli economy is not built to function alone. The economy of a country like Israel should be entirely centered in the Middle East, but in reality it is an economy that is half that of a developed country, half that of an undeveloped one. In its trade with the capitalist and industrialized countries, Israel generally supplies fruits, vegetables or flowers; its economy cannot be maintained sufficiently by this kind of production and foreign trade, nor even by polishing diamonds." He concludes this wonderfully original economic analysis by speaking of Israel's long dependency upon German reparations and its current reliance on money given "by the pro-Israel Jews of New York." It is absurd, he argues, to speak of Israel as "the spearhead of American imperialism, but it is a fact that Israel at present needs the support of the American Jews." However, the Arabs themselves have put Israel into a position in which she is "condemned—militarily and economically —to depend not on the governments of the imperialist states but on the Jewish minorities of those states, who to a large extent support the politics of those states."

Sartre goes on to chide those who claim that the Arabs started the war of 1967. And here the suspicion bred by his carefree analysis of the Israeli economy and the support of Israel by imperialist-minded Jews in the United States can no longer be repressed, and I ask myself: Did this influential thinker and prominent revolutionist know what he was saying? President Gamal Abdel Nasser was aware when he closed the Gulf of Aqaba and drove out the U.N. peacekeeping force that Israel had no choice

*"Sartre Looks at the Middle East Again: An Interview," *Midstream*, August–September 1969, pp. 37–48.

but to fight. Nasser not only threatened the very existence of Israel but defied the governments of France, Great Britain, and the United States, which had pledged themselves to keep Aqaba open. Nasser's friend Mohammed Heikal, Egypt's leading political journalist, wrote in May, before the war broke out, that Israel's security had been threatened and that it would now be forced to attack. Sartre says, "Those who claim that the Arabs started the war, that they are criminals, forget to consider the situation of the Palestinians, the absolutely insufferable situation of the Palestinians. They also forget that the Arabs from the beginning have been led by British maneuvers to take a negative attitude toward Israel, an attitude which has persisted since 1948, when an idiotic war was provoked."

Many Palestinians have suffered greatly, but it was not because of their suffering that Nasser went to war in 1967. Nasser didn't want them resettled; he kept them rotting in refugee camps and used them against Israel. The British did not create the Arab-Jewish conflict, though they may have aggravated it. If the Arab states did not deliberately exploit the Palestinians for political purposes, then the kindest interpretation of their conduct is that they were utterly incompetent. It is true that Israel might have done more for the refugees, over the years. The efforts made to indemnify those who had lost their lands and homes were far from adequate. Hannah Arendt used to argue that a part of the German reparations should have been set aside by Israel for the relief of the Palestinians. But this might have been construed to mean that what the Nazis had done to the Jews resembled what Zionism had done to the Arabs—a parallel no sane person would agree to. Still, it would have abated the strain if a large sum had been given to a neutral international agency for the payment of Palestinian claims. The Palestinian Conciliation Committee, a group created by the U.N. in 1948 to negotiate an Arab-Israeli peace settlement, put a preliminary valuation of $300 million on Arab-owned property. It is essential to add that most

Palestinian Arabs feared the consequences of accepting indemnities.

In any case, the British in 1948 did not provoke the invasion of Israel by its Arab neighbors. Egypt and the others sent in their troops to destroy the new state when the British Mandate ended. "One day at the Café de Flore," writes Raymond Aron, "Sartre and Simone de Beauvoir were loosing off their righteous wrath against the British. I pointed out that the latter had no easy task between the Jews and the Arabs, they had not created the Israeli-Arab conflict, they were trying to arbitrate it. At the time, Simone de Beauvoir and Sartre were always looking for a simple dividing line between angels and devils, and could see nothing except the cruelty (or imperialism) of the British and the sacred cause of the martyrs." More than twenty years later Sartre was still talking of British imperialism. A definition is a definition. Sartre is not conspicuously flexible. He has what I call the Larousse syndrome. All that a Parisian needs to know about Eskimos or their kayaks he can find in his Larousse, where a little yellow man dressed in furs sits in his kayak. De Gaulle often offended the Russians by using the expression "from the Atlantic to the Urals" to describe Europe, Ambassador Charles E. Bohlen says in his memoirs.* This was how Europe was described in the *Petit Larousse* of 1907. There is sometimes a bit of a lag in the French version of things. Sartre derives his definition of imperialism from Lenin. The substance of Lenin's pamphlet *Imperialism, the Highest Stage of Capitalism*, written in 1916, was drawn from John Atkinson Hobson's *Imperialism*, published in 1902. Truth is timeless, certainly, and one doesn't have to be up to date to be right, but in taking positions or advocating actions that may cost people their lives one should be as clear as possible about historical facts. Here the danger that "thinkers" can constitute for the rest of humanity begins to be very plain.

Witness to History (New York, 1973) .

In the 1969 interview, Sartre, whose attitudes are generally shared by the European left, sympathizes with Israel. At the same time, he wants a revolution in the Arab world. He expects that more popular or leftist Arab regimes would find Israel's existence easier to accept. Sartre is energetically directing the band, but the tunes that come out are not those in the score he has composed in his simplicity of heart. The Marxist-Leninist leaders of the Arab world were and remain even more hostile to Israel than the feudal princes of the oil kingdoms. Arab Marxists deny that Israel can produce a left, although Sartre insists that "the class struggle exists in Israel as it does elsewhere . . . and that consequently there are the elements of a left movement." However, he laments, "You cannot invite both Israelis and Arabs to an international conference. You can't because the Arabs don't want it." "But why always give in to the Arab boycott?" asks his interviewer. "Because," answers Sartre, "the left seems to have more sympathy for certain liberation movements—think of Algeria for us—than for a government or a country which up to these last years was not threatened the way it is now. The real problem for us was, 'What is going on in Algeria? What is going on in the Moroccan left? What does the Aswan Dam mean? Is Nasser really taking objectively Socialist steps in Egypt?' . . . Actually it is shameful not to invite the representatives of the Israeli left but if we invite them—let us not be hypocritical—that means not inviting the Arabs." In other words, there are millions of Arabs; they are politically big. Neither the State Department nor the Politburo nor Jean-Paul Sartre can afford to disregard them.

A new question is put to Sartre: Was the aim of the Arab states in 1948 and again in 1967 the extermination of the Jewish population in Israel? Yes, Sartre answers, but as a state. He elaborates. He knows Arabs—leftist Arabs, of course—quite well, and "all those I knew think of Israel as a state, not of Israel as a Jewish minority; on the contrary: 'We have to make a state that will be Arab

or Palestinian and Jewish—that's our business,' they say.
... The idea of some responsible political persons was to
suppress the state and not the Jews as a minority." To
this the interviewer replies that he was born in Alexan-
dria and lived in the Middle East for more than twenty-
five years and knows how minorities—the Copts, the Jews,
and others—are treated in Egypt. They are second-class
citizens, he says, "just as in the United States the only
full citizens are the white Protestants, in the Arab countries the only full citizens are Muslim Arabs."

Sartre agrees but also resists, shifting his argument.
The Egyptian fellah is not a full citizen, either. He is
illiterate; therefore citizenship is beyond his reach. Only
"certain powerful groups against which the Egyptian government has tried to fight" enjoy full citizenship. Below
them there is no category that has political rights. Having
said this, he admits that, "The problem of the minorities
is very often solved in the Middle East by massacre."
Sartre excuses the Jews from the charge of colonialism;
if they were colonialists and imperialists, he would be
constrained by his logic to call for their extermination,
for in his lengthy introduction to Frantz Fanon's *The
Wretched of the Earth* he exhorts oppressed backward
people to fall upon their exploiters and murder them.
Only by killing can the victims of imperialist exploitation
achieve freedom, self-respect, and manhood. They must
shoot down their white oppressors and redeem themselves
by bloodshed.

The blood is perhaps, like so much in Sartre, imag-
inary. From his record, we know that there is blood and
blood, for in 1949 the French writer David Rousset, who
had been sent by the Germans to Buchenwald, drafted a
manifesto condemning the destruction of millions of prisoners in Russian concentration camps, and Sartre refused
to sign it. He said that by signing he would be justifying
or strengthening American imperialism.

He speaks in his interview of the great value conferred
upon Jews by their suffering, by their "heritage of permanent persecution," which is infinitely precious. But

it is precisely because they have been so dreadfully persecuted that "the State of Israel must set an example; we have to demand more from this state than from others." Now, how is this special and precious destiny to be reconciled with the anti-Semitism of the Socialist countries of Eastern Europe? For in Sartre's eyes these are precious and special, too, and the inconsistency demands explanation. Jealous of their sovereignty, these Socialist—or so-called Socialist—countries see their own Jewish communities as having a dual affiliation. They are not quite like other citizens, since they have the choice of going to Israel—Israel, with its Law of Return, has guaranteed to receive them. This, says Sartre, encourages anti-Semitism. "If a Soviet or Rumanian citizen, even now only too much tempted by anti-Semitism, does not have the right to leave the country except under very specific circumstances, while a Rumanian Jew, on the contrary, can call himself both Rumanian and Israeli, according to his choice, the non-Jew will think both that these people are more favored than he is, and also that they are not loyal. At the same time, the government looks upon them with hostility, claiming that from the moment they choose or can choose Israel, they are not Socialists. Whether they are wrong or right I don't know, but what I am sure of is that this kind of Zionist activity is a very serious thing. I would think that we would have to recognize Israel's right, as a sovereign state, to accept all the Jews who may want to come to her, but that she should not make militant Zionist politics abroad." What does this indicate? For one thing, massive ignorance of the conditions of life in Eastern Europe. Soviet citizens live under an immense number of restrictions. They do not move about freely in Russia, much less emigrate. Sartre is saying, then, that non-Jews in Russia are hostile toward Jews because Jews could go to Israel *if* the government allowed them to emigrate. But he is also saying that the Jews are oppressed and wish to leave, and therefore they are not loyal Socialists and good Soviet citizens.

This is, indeed, the Swiftian philosopher extracting

sunshine from cucumbers and getting spiders to manufacture silks.

Nadezhda Mandelstam, the poet's widow, who knows Socialist countries better than Sartre does, says anti-Semitism in Russia is a state product that is "propagated from above and brews in the caldron known as the *apparat*." Andrei Sinyavsky does not agree that anti-Semitism is entirely imposed from above. In the popular consciousness, he explains, the Jew is an evil spirit, a devil who has got into the body of Russia and makes everything go wrong. The Russian peasant has "known" for some time that Lenin was a Jew, Stalin a Georgian Jew. In prison, Sinyavsky heard even Leo Tolstoi identified as a Jew.

What is "known" in civilized countries, what people may be assumed to "know," is a great mystery. Recently, a survivor of Auschwitz who now lives in Chicago had occasion to testify before a grand jury and was asked by the jury foreman, "Why were you sent to this prison camp? What crime did you commit?" "No crime, there was no trial." "That can't be a truthful answer," said the foreman. "When people go to jail it's because of something they've done. You must have had a criminal record in the old country." When I read Sartre on the Jewish question, I am less surprised by the remoteness of this grand juror's mind. I am, if anything, surprised at myself and at my own assumptions. A great deal of intelligence can be invested in ignorance when the need for illusion is deep.

The putative friends of Israel are always urging that it set the world a moral example: "We have to demand more from this state." Not all states are exposed to this demand. One of de Gaulle's ministers, when he spoke of France's friends at a Cabinet meeting, was interrupted by the General. A nation has interests, not friends, he corrected him. How would de Gaulle have fared in 1940 if the British had not befriended him? Nations do, at times, have friends as well as interests. True, there were (and are) tough people in the Pentagon, the State Department, and the Congress who preferred to think of interests, not friendships. But America has in its own loose way entertained moral sentiments—or would have felt ill at ease without them. Between 1950 and June 1975 the United States contributed more than $600 million to the United Nations Relief and Works Agency fund for the relief of Palestinian refugees. Israel gave more than $6 million. The Soviet Union contributed nothing, the Chinese nothing, the Algerian government, so concerned about the Palestinians, nothing.

But Sartre and others apparently want the Jews to be exceptionally exceptional. Perhaps the Jews have themselves created such expectations. Israel has made extraordinary efforts to be democratic, equitable, reasonable, capable of change. It has, in fact, transformed its Jews. In Hitler's Europe, they were led to the slaughter; in 1948, the survivors became formidable fighters. Landless in exile, they turned into farmers. The Mamlukes had decreed that the Palestinian coastal plain should be a desert; they made a garden of it. Obviously, the Jews accepted a historic responsibility to be exceptional. They have been held to this; they have held themselves to it. Now the question is whether more cannot be demanded from other peoples. On the others, no such demands are made. I sometimes wonder why it is impossible for Western intellectuals (and especially the French, who enjoy such prestige in Syria, Lebanon, and Egypt and who have relations with the Arab left in these countries) to say to the Arabs, "We have to demand also more from you. You, too—the Marxists among you in particular—must try to do something for brotherhood and make peace with the Jews, for they have suffered monstrously, in Christian Europe and under Islam. Israel occupies about one-sixth of one per cent of the lands you call Arab. Isn't it possible to adjust the traditions of Islam—to reinterpret, to change emphasis, so as to accept this trifling occupancy? A great civilization should be capable of humane and generous flexibility. The destruction of Israel will do you no good. Let the Jews live, in their small state." But it must be culturally disrespectful to ask people to change their attitudes, even slightly. In any case, Sartre has not said such things. He has had revolution—glorious, ineffable revolution—to think of. An explosion of a hundred million Arabs can tear a huge hole in the rotting bourgeois structure. After an ecstatic time of murder will come peace and justice. The fellahin, their manhood recovered, will learn to read and be citizens, et cetera. "It is shameful not to invite the representatives of the Israeli left but if we invite them—let us not be hypocritical—that means not inviting Arabs," said Sartre.

FINAL walks in Jerusalem. More farewell than sightseeing. The cold rains that streak down are sometimes oddly localized so that at no great distance
from the rain cloud the sky can be clear. My brother
Sam, who is visiting Jerusalem with his wife, astonishes
me: he turns up at my door. In the States this would
never happen. We live at opposite ends of Chicago and
make appointments on the telephone for lunch or dinner.
Our routines take us in different directions. So it must
be thirty years or more since we faced each other at
leisure on an ordinary morning. We are silently amused.
My brother's smile is jaunty and exceptionally communi-
cative. We look at each other. Except for the eyes, we are
entirely changed. We have mainly this brown-eyed evidence that there is an age-free essence in each of us, un-
altered. The rest is wrinkles. And why shouldn't we smile?

Cousin Nota Gordon comes up from Tel Aviv later
in the week, and then there are three family faces in one
room. Nota's complexion is different from ours, it has
pale-brown tones. Besides, he wears a cap, Soviet style,
and there are gold crowns on some of his teeth. But we
are obviously from the same genetic pool. Nota is manu-
facturing sweaters in Tel Aviv on knitting machines im-
ported from Italy. That sounds grand but isn't. The savings of twenty-five years were spent to buy emigration
permits for his wife, his two sons, and his sisters. He
arrived penniless in Israel and borrowed money to start
a business.

A plain man, he leads a plain life, like all the Riga

cousins. His flat is small and crowded with old-fashioned furniture. Our cousin Liza and her husband, Westreich, own a grocery; it is no bigger than a pantry but it keeps them on their feet ten hours a day. Cousin Bella, in Latvia a medical worker of some sort, is here a department store cashier. Her son, an engineer, does electronic work for Sony. Bella tells me of one of our cousins who now lives with her husband in Geneva. During the German occupation of Riga this cousin and her sister were slave laborers in a factory that made army uniforms. Before the Germans retreated they exhumed thousands of bodies from the mass graves and burned them. A sudden sensitivity about evidence. The two young girls were among the hundreds forced to dig up putrid corpses and put them in the flames. The younger sister sickened and died.

Our European cousins who have known arrest, deportation, massacre, and war are glad to lead ordinary lives. They have, curiously, more rest in their souls than the American side of the family; they are less secure but also less fretful. Observing their temper and their ways, I wonder about the effects of limitless expectation on the American sense of reality. What some of the Russian dissidents observe in capitalist democracy, in American society, is what human nature can be when it is provided with opportunities for expansion. They think that since the end of World War II the Americans haven't wanted to hear, haven't wanted to see anything that would interfere with these opportunities. As some of these Russian intellectuals see it, the wealthy, productive, exuberant American world—for Henry James was right, and America is more a world than a country—has wanted only to enjoy its own national development and the privileges of personal development. Happy with its money and its machines, happy in its opportunities for travel and shopping, its sexual opportunities and its entertainments, it was willing to let Stalin have the Poles, the Hungarians, the Rumanians, the Czechs. The charge is that we paid off the Communist dictatorships to let us be, and that we still do this by the form of appeasement we choose to call détente. Solzhenitsyn accuses the West of believing that liberty is a once-and-for-all acquisition. As a result, ours is no longer the liberty of heroism and virtue but a stunted and specious thing, "full of tinsel, affluence, and emptiness," says Solzhenitsyn. And he adds, "So you have entered the era of calculation. You are no longer capable of making sacrifices for this shadow of the liberty that once existed, only compromises. Let that territory over there be abandoned, you say, as long as prosperity persists for a while on the soil where we set our feet."

When I was a graduate student in anthropology, it was my immature ambition to investigate bands of Eskimos who were reported to have chosen to starve rather than eat foods that were abundant but under taboo. How much, I asked myself, did people yield to culture or to their lifelong preoccupations, and at what point would the animal need to survive break through the restraints of custom and belief? I suspected then that among primitive peoples the objective facts counted for less. But I'm not at all certain now that civilized minds are more flexible and capable of grasping reality, or that they have livelier, more intelligent reactions to the threat of extinction. I grant that as an American I am more subject to illusion than my cousins. But will the Israeli veterans of hardships, massacres, and wars know how to save themselves? Has the experience of crisis taught them what to do? I have read writers on the Holocaust who made the most grave criticisms of European Jewry, arguing that they doomed themselves by their unwillingness to surrender their comfortable ways, their property, their passive habits, their acceptance of bureaucracy, and were led to slaughter unresisting. I do not see the point of scolding the dead. But if history is indeed a nightmare, as Karl Marx and James Joyce said, it is time for the Jews, a historical people, to rouse themselves, to burst from historical sleep. And Israel's political leaders do not seem to me to be awake. I sometimes think there are two Israels. The real one is territorially insignificant. The other, the mental Israel, is immense, a country inestimably important, playing a major role in the world, as broad as all history—and perhaps as deep as sleep.

A family drive. My brother, his wife, Shimshon, one of their religious, philanthropic friends, Cousin Nota, and I visit the West Bank. We take the bypass and avoid Bethlehem and its Christmas crowds. We drive toward Hebron. A Judean sun over the ribbed fields, the russet colors of winter, mild gold mixed with the light, and white stone terraces everywhere. Many times cleared, the ground goes on giving birth to stones; waves of earth bring forth more stone. The ancient fields are very small.

From these villages come the Arab construction workers you see in Jerusalem. There are leftists, and even some old Zionists, who complain of this. They say that Jewish labor built Israel but that now the Arabs do all the disagreeable jobs and form an exploited class of bottom dogs. But this is probably not how the Arab laborers see themselves. Their wages have risen, and there is no precedent for the prosperity they enjoy. Pan-Arabism has undoubtedly influenced them; they are nationalists and would vote for self-determination if elections were to be held. They are, however, laborers and wage earners, not terrorists. Those who make angry demonstrations, who throw the stones, challenge the occupation, and plant bombs in Jerusalem and other cities are the young, many of them adolescents. They have their counterparts among the Israeli militants of the Gush Emunim movement—young men and women who are determined for religious reasons to colonize the West Bank. Their settlements are held by some to imply a rejection of Zionism, for the Zionist pioneers were satisfied with a sanctuary and did not try to recover the Promised Land. Unlike the religious irredentists, they sought sparsely populated places for settlement and for the most part avoided Arab towns. The early kibbutzim were founded in the swamps and the sand dunes. Arabs in old communities like Hebron, Jericho, and Jenin now feel threatened by Jewish settlers bent on realizing God's promise. Shimshon, who is a retired Chicago businessman, very observant and busy in Jewish affairs, takes us to Gush Etzion and proudly shows us the yeshiva, a newly built fortress of Orthodoxy. Near this place, before World War II, a Jewish colony was attacked and wiped out by the Arabs. Descendants of the victims are farming nearby. Sturdy, rugged people, they are undoubtedly armed and would not be easy to move out. Their new buildings of concrete have a grim Maginot Line look about them. The young men wear skullcaps but their frames are big and their forearms thick with muscle. Their beards are far from tame and rabbinical; they bristle. We leave these pillbox dwellings and go on to Kiryat Arba to be shown the apartment buildings built by Israelis—with the permission of the government, I suppose. Shimshon approves of them. The building sites are still raw; neither grass nor trees have as yet been planted. Washing is looped, Mediterranean style, from lines sagging under the windows. On the newly laid paths, isolated-looking kids pedal their tricycles. It's when I see the children on their bikes that I feel most uneasy, knowing how much madness there is just over the horizon.

In Lebanon, ten minutes away by jet, armed gangs kill hundreds of people weekly. On your television set you can see murders committed. Corpses are tied to automobile bumpers and dragged through the streets. The bottom has fallen out of Beirut. Reporters say that Christians and Muslims no longer seem to know whom they are shooting, or why.

The more difficult the position of the Rabin government becomes, the more heat it has to take from the religious settlers and their supporters. The Cabinet is sharply divided, and the government is too weak to deal with the Gush Emunim militants. It has not been able to dislodge them from places like Sebastia and Kadum, where they live as squatters at the very center of the occupied West Bank.

Just after the Jordanians had been driven out in 1967

I visited these parts with Sydney Gruson, of *The New York Times*. Having won their war on this front, young Israeli soldiers took a holiday and went joyriding in Arab automobiles. Two days later, on their way to the battle for the Golan Heights, they were still celebrating. In open tank turrets as they ground through Tiberias they held store-window dummies dressed in fluttering Arab skirts and blouses with costume jewelry swinging. I had arrived hours before them. That was easy enough. In Tel Aviv I simply stopped a cab, showed my press credentials, and said, "Take me to the Galilee." The cabbies, veterans of 1948 and 1956, now too old to fight, were delighted to drive you to the front for a look at the action.

On the West Bank I traveled in style, for Gruson had his own car. The *Times* impressed me with the efficiency of its organization. Its team was headed by Gruson, who divided the work and gave out assignments. The rest of us were haphazard amateurs with few connections. Gruson is an agreeable man, breezily professional. He has replied to the note I sent him some weeks ago enclosing a copy of a statement—admiring, even worshipful—that Anwar Sadat had written on Hitler in 1953. Gruson thanked me and said he was having the document checked. Somewhere in his files he had a picture of the two of us "at the front," he added. In the fields near Jerusalem, I remember, soldiers were prodding the soil for land mines, marking out the safe paths with strips of rag.

THE mood of Jacob Leib Talmon is at the same time fervent and depressed. An energetic and dramatic talker, he draws his wide historical knowledge into the conversation. There is a certain plump, professorial propriety about him. He is finely dressed, tie well chosen—he is not one of your open-at-the-throat, bushy Israeli types. The conversation is serious—"tormented" is perhaps a better word for it. He expresses comprehensively what I have been hearing for months—every suspicion, doubt, and fear. The crisis is severe. An Israeli friend has more than once warned me, "For God's sake, don't be carried away by what the intellectuals say here. You of all people should know better." I remember this warning now, but at the same time I can see how deeply disturbed the Professor is, how his heart is being wrung. He speaks of Jewish history, European history, world history, but in the midst of one of his academic sentences he breaks off and says, "Didn't Hitler after all win? As far as the Jews are concerned? At least one-third of the six million who died in the camps were the best hope of a future Israel—Zionists, liberal democrats, highly trained and accomplished. And they were destroyed, gassed and burnt, these millions, went up in smoke. The 'Jewish Question' itself went up in smoke. The Oriental Jews who have come here are admirable in their own way, but they are without the modern skills that are so badly needed. Yes, while the Jews suffered under Hitler the conscience of the world was aware of them, but when they were dead that awareness also died. Ah, before

171

1939, the Jews of Central and Eastern Europe created a rich, vital civilization—a culture, a literature, institutions. It all went into the graves and into the ovens. And when it was gone there were only the synagogues to give cohesion to Jewish life in these increasingly secular times. This is one reason for the success of Jewish clericalism in Israel. Our politicians are obliged to make use of everything that can draw us together."

Professor Talmon, whose subject is European political history, ranges far beyond Israel. When he speaks of the new forms of Israeli nationalism, he mentions also the French and Slavophile varieties. Integral nationalism, as he calls it, amounts to one thing: the power of the dead over the living. He intensely fears fanatical nationalist extremism in Israel. We discuss the debate over future frontiers. It is lunacy, he says, to carry the argument back to the Judaism of the Bronze Age and to invoke the enmity of the Amalekites and the Edomites, to claim eternal rights—past, present, and future—in the Holy Land and to combine eschatological visions with modern arms. What worries Talmon is that elsewhere such movements have invariably been intensely anti-Semitic. Mystical nationalists in Israel are using the language of a holy war. The Arab extremists also call for a holy war, a *jihad.* The situation is explosive. Jewish survival is not only threatened by Arab enemies but undermined from within, says Talmon.

After the victory of 1967 Israel could briefly think of itself as a military power. It could think of itself also, says Talmon in a manuscript he sent me, "as one of the few countries in the contemporary jaded world with a sense of purpose."* This last I consider of first importance. The Israelis had war, and not the moral equivalent of war William James was looking for, to give them firmness. They had, in their concern for the decay of civilization and in their pride (pride and concern in equal proportions), something to teach the world. The stunned

*"Reflections of an Historian in Jerusalem," *Encounter,* May 1976.

remnant that had crept from Auschwitz had demonstrated that they could farm a barren land, industrialize it, build cities, make a society, do research, philosophize, write books, sustain a great moral tradition, and, finally, create an army of tough fighters.

The 1973 war badly damaged their confidence. The Egyptians crossed the Suez Canal. Suddenly the abyss opened again. France and England abandoned Israel. The U.N.-bloc vote revived the feeling that she "shall not be reckoned among the nations." While Israel fought for life, debaters weighed her sins and especially the problem of the Palestinians. In this disorderly century refugees have fled from many countries. In India, in Africa, in Europe, millions of human beings have been put to flight, transported, enslaved, stampeded over the borders, left to starve, but only the case of the Palestinians is held permanently open. Where Israel is concerned, the world swells with moral consciousness. Moral judgment, a wraith in Europe, becomes a full-blooded giant when Israel and the Palestinians are mentioned. Is this because Israel has assumed the responsibilities of a liberal democracy? Is it for other reasons? What Switzerland is to winter holidays and the Dalmatian coast to summer tourists, Israel and the Palestinians are to the West's need for justice—a sort of moral resort area.

The right of Israel to exist, Talmon says, has to be won by special exertions, "by some special atonement, through being better than others." This is Israel's most persistent torment and paradox. "We demand more from this state," says Sartre. But since Israel's sovereignty is questioned and world opinion is not ready to agree that it is indeed a country like other countries, to demand more is cruelly absurd. Israel is, in Talmon's view, becoming a "ghetto state." Is it from a "ghetto state" that more should be demanded? It will not be easy to trace this unlovely paradox to its origins. Jewish moral traditions themselves possibly have something to do with it. On the other hand, many European radicals have, it seems to me, deferred moral expectations and choose to

predict that history, itself a sort of moral engine, will
develop just societies through class struggle and revolution. They do not ask that the African peasant or the
illiterate fellah should be moral by our standards (by our
past standards, one should say). But some of them do
appear to believe that the Jews, with their precious and
refining record of suffering, have a unique obligation to
hold up the moral burdens everyone else has dumped.

So, then, says Talmon, Israel, which was briefly so
proud and confident after 1967, has overnight been re-
duced to beggary while its mortal enemies with their
petro-dollars have become the world's most potent bankers and investors. The ambassadors of proud countries
grovel before the petroleum princes. American, British,
and French businessmen press to sell them computers,
nuclear reactors, missiles, planes, and entire industrial
systems. Only the United States can, for the time being,
afford to support Israel. The gentle, overwrought Professor Talmon, trying to filter this flood of causes and
effects through his learned mind, is at one instant men-
tioning the Hasmoneans and the Romans, and the next
Marx and Lenin or Charles Maurras, Auguste-Maurice
Barrès, and the Catholic Church. Would matters be
easier for him if he didn't think so many things? Although
he is the source of these speeding thoughts, he seems at
times to be their target.

Professor Talmon, toward the end of our conversation,
speaks about Israel and world Jewry. The fate of Jewry in
Israel and in the Diaspora is so closely linked, he says,
that the destruction of Israel would bring with it the destruction of "corporate Jewish existence all over the
world, and a catastrophe that might overtake U.S.
Jewry."

A final session with Moshe the masseur. His brief talks on anatomy will be missed, not because they bring new information (he repeats himself) but because I like his fresh-and-faded middle-aged boyishness and innocence and his vatic attitude toward that temple the body. He opens his peeling satchel and lays out his oil bottles, he soaks towels in scalding water to apply to my back, he tucks a bolster under my ankles, and while he kneads me he explains his techniques, reveals the mysterious relations between the muscles and the organs. It's all terrifically up to date, scientific, wonderful; at the same time it is ancient, Aesculapian. When he asks me about masseurs in literature, I can think only of the blind man in Rayner Heppenstall's novel *The Blaze of Noon*. And vaguely someone in a Japanese novel. Was it Junichiro Tanizaki's *Diary of a Mad Old Man*? Tanizaki has drawn some of the most extraordinary hypochondriacs in fiction. His wretched, perverse, half-hallucinated old sexpot is wonderfully persistent; the cunning daughter-in-law with whom he is infatuated extracts money from him. He had a nurse, but was there also a masseur? No, it was in Tanizaki's *A Blind Man's Tale* that the masseur I am thinking of appears. But I describe Japanese massage to Moshe. You do not undress; the treatment is given through the clothing. "Clever," says Moshe. "Through the clothes there is no friction." He has never heard of the Heppenstall book and makes a note of the title. He speaks of the future of massage in this country—massage as a career for young

175

Israelis. He tells me about a young man who was attracted to the profession. The boy's father came storming into the bathhouse where Moshe works. "He upbraided me," says Moshe. "But I mollified him. I persuaded him that it was an art, and a real calling. He began to see the light."

At last Moshe puts on his winter coat and says, "I'm afraid this is good-by." We have a few shots of genuine Rumanian *zuica*. You can buy adequate *zuica* in Jerusalem. You buy Polish herb-flavored vodka or Stolichnaya from the Armenian dealer across the valley. But nothing like this clear *zuica* from the Carpathians is obtainable here. I share this rare quintessence of plums with Moshe because I am sorry to see him go. I wonder what it takes to remain so eager well into middle age. The hair thins but the feelings are fresh. He hopes I won't forget to practice tracing the numbers from one through nine with my head. There's nothing better for a stiff neck. If he hears of a good masseur in Chicago, he will send the name on to me.

LATE in the afternoon we put out all the wine, the brandy, and the booze, the olives, nuts, cheeses, sausages, and biscuits. Departing visitors sometimes throw a farewell bash. Isaac Stern and his wife did, and before them Alexander Schneider. Nothing that resembles the American cocktail party, where people in pairs stand talking, trying to hear each other in the uproar. I've often thought that some hearing-aid manufacturer might make a fortune selling private-communication sets for cocktail parties and dinner tables. Here everyone sits eating and drinking and there is generally a single conversation. Alexandra's mathematical colleagues are here with their wives; Dennis Silk comes, and we exchange gifts—I get his copy of Professor Werblowsky's *Joseph Karo,* a book I covet; he gets my reversible corduroy raincoat from Milan, because I know that he fancies it. Peter Halban, who runs the Mishkenot, turns up, and Hannah, Ariane, and Anny, who work there; David and Shula Shahar come. Walter Hasenklever is here, on his way back from the Far East; and our friends the Daleskis; and Mr. and Mrs. Teddy Kollek. Punctilious Kollek never drops a stitch: we were his guests, we are leaving, he is here to say good-by. To mellow the sad occasion, we eat everything in sight and empty the bottles.

During the night there is more sighing than sleeping. Thinking, What will it be like not to see John Auerbach and Nola, my dear friends from Kibbutz Sdot Yam in Caesarea? The cab is coming before dawn, and we get up, still heartsick about leaving, to finish the packing. We never did learn the trick of lighting the oven, and still heat the buns atop the toaster, often burning them. Alexandra opens the door to take a last look at Mount Zion. Upstairs there is a difficulty. The helpful management in its zeal has telephoned twice for taxis, and there are two drivers. I make useless apologies. Together the drivers calmly work out an arrangement. One of them with good nature wishes us a safe journey and goes.

As we start for the Ben-Gurion Airport, a huge soft cloud of smoke bursts from the engine of the old Mercedes. Alexandra says, "Ah, we're going to miss the plane," brightening. I couldn't bear to return to the empties, the dishes, and the papers heaped on every table. But the driver knows exactly what to do under the hood. There is nothing to discuss. He fiddles with a wire. She runs. In five minutes we are out of the city and rushing down the mountainside.

ON a Saturday flight there are no Hasidim. Over the Mediterranean we drink coffee. The suave engines have us in their power and we hang over what we know is beauty—beauty above and below us, a deeper and a lighter blue—feeling no speed, no motion. We are suspended and we hear one thing after another, and receive one thing after another to drink. We suck orange juice through straws from a covered paper container while we pass over Cyprus—or is it Crete? Did the pilot also mention the Adriatic? Then come the summits of the Alps with their snows, and the cumulus clouds. Some of the passengers are popping away with flashbulbs. I remember how Ruskin fulminated against the new breed of citizens and sightseers. "You have despised Art. . . . You have despised nature; that is to say, all the deep and sacred sensations of natural scenery. . . . You have put a railroad bridge over the fall of Schaffhausen. . . . There is not a quiet valley in England that you have not filled with bellowing fire. . . ."

The clouds are no longer cumulus and golden but lie flat and gray under us, like woollens, between the high blue continuing northward and the chill ground. We go through this gray cover and there is wintry England, dark green and parklike. And London's domestic, comfortable gloom, good therapy for perturbed spirits. We go to Durrant's Hotel, on George Street.

On George Street the view of Mount Zion is replaced by the Victorian walls and windows of the museum opposite. We can see into the side street where Captain

Frederick Marryat, author of *Mr. Midshipman Easy*, wrote his novels. To help settle the dither of travel we have our bottle of *zuica*, still half full—good for jimjams and trailing regrets. We've carried it well wrapped in a burlap shopping bag.

Then we go out. The great Saturday crowd in Oxford Street. Terrorist bombs are nearly as likely to go off here as on Jaffa Road. Alexandra wants a mathematics book, so we take the bus to Foyle's, on Charing Cross Road. Awful, all these books! But I buy a few more to add to my Middle East library. With our packages we loiter toward Piccadilly and the movies—if one can be said to loiter in this cold. A street entertainer in clown's paint is doing a dancing tramp routine to music from two speakers provided by himself, juggling his bowler hat. He can only slow the crowd, which seems largely non-English (Asiatics, West Indians, Spaniards), not hold it. We are looking at the marquees for a suitable moving picture. It's too cold for sightseeing, too early for dinner.

We decide on a Tom Stoppard movie; it is terrible. What we really wanted was to come in from the chill gull-gray street, eat chocolate in the dark, and watch things harmlessly whirling while we recovered a bit from the jet lag. In other circumstances I might not have minded the badness of the film quite so much. But after three months in the earnest climate of Jerusalem we are not ready to let anything as feeble as this into our heads. It is a case of cultural shock. The emptiness of the picture is sobering—numbing. It gives me a sense of the rapid ruin of any number of revolutions—egalitarian, sexual, aesthetic. They didn't last long, did they? They were serious, they were necessary, but they were very quickly brought to the boutique level. The great enemy of progressive ideals is not the Establishment but the limitless dullness of those who take them up.

Life in Israel is far from enviable, yet there is a clear purpose in it. People are fighting for the society they have created, and for life and honor. Israel is too small and too special a case to be grouped with the democracies of the West or contrasted with them. It, too, is in disorder, with a rising crime rate, a weak government, and political parties pulling every which way. The wars, Israelis will sometimes tell you, have kept off the danger of Levantine slackness and corruption. But the connection of democratic nations with the civilization that formed them is growing loose and queer. They seem to have forgotten what they are about. They seem to be experimenting or gambling with their liberties, unwittingly preparing themselves for totalitarianism, or perhaps not quite consciously willing it. Joseph A. Schumpeter, in *Capitalism, Socialism, and Democracy*, is aware of a prevailing hostility to capitalism in capitalist countries. To condemn it and to declare one's aversion to it has become "almost a requirement of the etiquette of discussion," he says. Those who know totalitarian societies are wondering when, if ever, Western liberalism will recognize its danger. This is what Solzhenitsyn sees as the spiritual crisis of the West. He says, "You have a feeling that the democracies can survive, but you aren't certain. The democracies are islands lost in the immense river of history. The water never stops rising."

IN London we visit Elie Kedourie and his wife. She is Sylvia Haim, a well-known Arabic scholar—dark-haired, a lovely round-faced woman. She brings us tea and cake, and joins the conversation. Kedourie is tall, slightly stooped, hair cut short. I've read two of his books, *The Chatham House Version* and *Arabic Political Memoirs*, and am deeply impressed. He writes without advocacy or rhetorical color and is master of his tangled and often bloody subject. I once heard my friend Edward Shils say that the intellectual life was the most passionate life a human being could lead; I think of this when I consider what a man like Kedourie does and ask myself whether I could bear the excitement and danger of his sort of career—the emotional danger and the mental responsibilities, I mean. When Kedourie looks at the new nationalism of the Third, or Developing, World of Asia and Africa, he sees something other than the ravages of Western imperialism as Hobson, Lenin, Toynbee, Sartre, and their disciples have described them. "Charges of economic exploitation are made, and the tyranny and arrogance of the Europeans are arraigned," Kedourie has written in a long essay.* "Yet it is a simple and obvious fact that these areas which are said to suffer from imperialism today have known nothing but alien rule throughout most of their history and that, until the coming of the Western powers, their experience of government was the insolence and greed of unchecked arbitrary

Nationalism in Asia and Africa (New York, 1970).

rule. It is not on these grounds therefore that the appearance of the West in Asia and Africa is to be deplored. A curse the West has indeed brought to the East but—and here lies the tragedy—not intentionally; indeed the curse was considered—and still is by many—a precious boon, the most precious that the West could confer on the East in expiation of its supposed sins; and the curse itself is as potent in its maleficence in the West as it is in the East. A rash, a malady, an infection spreading from Western Europe through the Balkans, the Ottoman Empire, India, the Far East, and Africa, eating up the fabric of settled society to leave it weakened and defenceless before ignorant and unscrupulous adventurers for further horror and atrocity: such are the terms to describe what the West has done to the rest of the world, not wilfully or knowingly, but mostly out of excellent intentions and by example of its prestige and prosperity." Political theory was the most devastating export of the West: constitutions and political parties, Western style, the concept of class struggle, plans for the reorganization of society on the Western model. What have the results of this been? Kedourie describes the attitudes that have developed with these words: "Resentment and impatience, the depravity of the rich and the virtue of the poor, the guilt of Europe and the innocence of Asia and Africa, salvation through violence, the coming reign of universal love: these are the elements of the thought of Sultan Galiev and Li Tachao, of Ikki Kita, Michel Aflaq, and Frantz Fanon. This theory is now the most popular and influential one in Asia and Africa. It is Europe's latest gift to the world. As Karl Marx remarked, theory itself becomes a material force when it has seized the masses; and with the printing press, the transistor, the television—those other gifts of Europe—it is easy now for theory, any theory, to seize the masses."

Sitting in Kedourie's parlor, we speak first of the Israeli-Arab conflict. In the Arab world, says Kedourie, power is now mainly in the hands of the petroleum princes of the Arabian Peninsula, and these are fervent

Muslims, whose thought has been least influenced by
Western ideas and who are most attached to the traditional view as to the place of the non-Muslim in an Islamic society. These fundamentalists would be at least
willing to acquiesce in a sovereign Jewish state established on what they would consider Muslim territory.
The West does not understand the Arab world; neither
does Israel, Kedourie says. He shows us an Egyptian
booklet made up largely of quotations from the Koran.
Its main theme is the holy war, and it was distributed to
officers and men before the outbreak of the October War.
In an introduction to this pamphlet, Lieutenant General
Sa'ad Shazli, who was then Egyptian Chief of Staff, says,
"My sons, officers and men! The Jews have overstepped
their bounds in injustice and conceit. And we sons of
Egypt have determined to set them back on their heels,
and to pry round their positions, killing and destroying
so as to wash away the shame of the 1967 defeat and to
restore our honor and pride. Kill them wherever you find
them and take heed that they do not deceive you, for they
are a treacherous people. They may feign surrender in
order to gain power over you, and kill you vilely. Kill
them and let not compassion or mercy for them seize
you!"

The fellah, Sartre argued, was deprived of the benefits
and rights of citizenship because he was illiterate. For
those who could not read, self-explanatory comic books
were distributed in 1967. I picked up copies of these in
the Sinai Desert. They contained anti-Semitic caricatures
of the Nazi type. I thought they had gone out with Julius
Streicher and *Der Stürmer*. But nothing disappears for
long. The Protocols of the Elders of Zion are distributed
in Arab countries in large new printings paid for in petro-
dollars. In the thirties, the Nazis won considerable support in the Middle East, and, earlier, French anti-Drey-
fusards had spread anti-Semitism in Syria and Lebanon,
where French culture was esteemed.

I ask Kedourie whether there are Arab intellectuals
who dissociate themselves to any extent from the tradi-

tional religious patriotism. It is useless to apply our Western measures and expectations to Arab intellectuals, he says. Another Arabist, Bernard Lewis, later tells me that the Arab intellectuals who speak most freely are to be found in Israel itself—in East Jerusalem and on the Israeli-occupied West Bank.

When I describe my conversation with Rabin to Kedourie, he agrees with the Prime Minister that territorial concession to the Arabs would be meaningless. They simply want the Jews out. He does not, however, accept Rabin's prediction that modernization will eventually soften the conflict. Successful modernization would make the Arab states feel strong, and this sense of greatly increased strength might diminish their willingness to resolve the conflict. The process of modernization also causes strains and tensions in societies and their political systems. The disorders resulting from modernization have not made the relations of the Arab states with Israel easier. Of course, the oil strength of the Arabs will diminish as other sources of energy are developed. The oil billionaires make sophisticated industrial purchases, but lack training, skill, and organization. In Algeria, for instance, a government of anti-French guerrillas, now immensely rich and quite free from responsibility to an electorate or the need to take world market conditions into account, has gone in for steel manufacture but so far has little to show for its investment.

As to Russia's objectives, in Kedourie's view the destruction of Israel is probably not one of them, but in order to prevent the United States from fastening its hold on the Middle East the Russians may let their armed clients go too far. What happens when sophisticated weapons are supplied to people with fighting appetites can be seen in Lebanon, where hundreds are killed weekly in incomprehensible street battles. The Russians may have intended to build "anti-imperialist" units in Lebanon, but their arms were used to attack the Christians. Ferocity and eagerness to kill are not easily controlled by political strategies.

It would be in Israel's interest to deal with the Arab states separately, says Kedourie. Coalitions are sometimes fatally cumbersome in negotiations. Differences within the German-Austro-Hungarian coalition in the Great War impeded peace efforts. The Arab nations are even more difficult in this respect. A superpower might, if it wished, simplify negotiations. But the Russians seem to have no desire for peaceful and orderly settlements. As for the Americans, it would be hard to give a coherent description of their policies.

When the Jews decided, through Zionism, to "go political," they didn't know what they were getting into. To their historical difficulties were added the troubles of a small state facing the storms of savage hostility.

Kedourie says nothing off the top of his head. His judgments are thoroughly considered. And he is not optimistic.

THIS, then, is what I bring to Chicago with me on our return.

The big winter-gray Chicago scene—ashen, with black strokes. In winter it takes on a kind of mineral character. After so many years I can still not believe that the causes of this are entirely natural but always suspect the presence of a grim power whose materials are streets, bungalows, tenements, naked ironwork, grit, wind—an enchanter whose idea is that everyone should take the city to be material, practical, all hustle. But this grim power is also a comedian, absurdist, ironist, and relishes Chicago's "realism"; he disguises his darkest fantasies in its materiality, in building, paving, drainage, engineering, banking, electronics.

We pile our bags into the front of a cab and ride off, the sharp tooth of the meter clicking. The papers report a new Chicago swindle: drivers unseal and tamper with their meters. You learn to live with such practices. You aren't duped (point of honor!) but you go along. Resistance is time-consuming, emotionally wasteful. Worse than crookery is the furious stink of the cab, a mixture of personal emanations and Oriental spices. We open the windows. Well, we're back, riding through the bungalow belt. Who knows how many brick bungalows there are in Chicago—a galactic number. There must be a single blueprint for them all: so much concrete, so many gingersnap bricks, a living room, dining room, two bedrooms, kitchen, porch, back yard, and garage. Below, a den or rumpus room. And wall-to-wall everything, and the drapes, and the Venetian blinds, the deep freeze, TV, washer and dryer, flueless fireplace—plainness, regularity, family attachments, dollar worries, fear of crime, acceptance of routine. We ride for twenty minutes through these bungalow blocks, silent, no need to say what we are thinking: the case states itself. Along the lake is the other Chicago, the giant high-rise apartment houses that face the water. Gray now, the lake will go blue when the sun shows.

And here it is again—same conditions, same questions and challenges as before, same carpets, books, sticks of furniture. In the morning, while the kettle boils, you turn the switch of the radio and hear the same programs, news broadcasters, commercials. The Talman Federal Savings & Loan, to please its Czech and Slovak depositors, seems to favor Smetana and Dvořák; you listen to "The Moldau" and the "Slavonic Dances" oftener than you might like. You hear, too, what all announcers refer to as "cultural programming," sponsored by wine and cheese shops, by hi-fi shops, and by ethnic restaurants bringing "Continental dining" to "Chicagoland." Always "Chicagoland," an enchanted place like Alice's Wonderland or the fairy tales' never-never land. Though it looks, at times, like the doughboys' no-man's-land. It was Colonel McCormick who gave the city this touch of poetry. He had many tony ideas. If you examine closely the façade of the Tribune Tower, you find that it contains fragments of the Acropolis, the Pyramids, the Great Wall of China, the Roman Colosseum, and of famous cathedrals and palaces: the Colonel's Tower incorporates, consummates, and transcends them all.

So the radio crackles with commercials for Peking duck and French "fondoo" dishes, and the names of wines, together with all of the world's disasters and outrages. And here, just as we left them, are books, papers, and phonograph records, and bundles of letters, and parcels, magazines, and manuscripts. Impossible to keep up with correspondence. Oscar Wilde said he had known a promising young man who had ruined himself through the vice of answering letters. Impossible to get through this midden of papers, plus the two or three books that arrive daily. At the university, I have a course to teach with David Grene on the long stories or short novels of Tolstoi: *Master and Man, Hadji Murád, Ivan Ilyich, Father Sergius*. I'm obliged, thank God, to read these masterpieces first. And also the *Odyssey*, for Grene has often invited me to do Homer in Greek with him. I attend two sessions of his tutorial, stumbling behind the skillful students. We do the Fifth Book. Odysseus leaves Calypso, putting the raft he had built into the "sacred sea." Poseidon, catching sight of him, stirs the waters into a frightful storm with his trident; Ino of the slender ankles comes to despairing Odysseus and gives him her veil and tells him to swim through the tempest. What can be more beautiful, more stirring than this—Odysseus praying in his weariness to the river god, who slows the current for him and lets him come to shore. So Odysseus comes to shore, the skin torn from his hands, the sea water gushing from his mouth and nostrils. He breathes again, and some warmth rallies in his heart.

But I am not able to make room for Homer beside my preoccupation with Israel. I read again the Samuel Butler *Odyssey*, which I know best, and then the beautiful T. E. Lawrence translation, and Lawrence sends me back to the Middle East, for I have recently read Elie Kedourie's essay on the capture of Damascus in 1918 and the role played by Lawrence in that event. I've always liked *The Mint* best of Lawrence's books, never doubting its truthfulness; it is the work of a man who has stripped himself down. The man who wrote *Seven Pillars* was, I always suspected, padded out, costumed, mixing romance with politics, attitudinizing. According to Kedourie, the account given by Lawrence of the taking of Damascus is quite simply untrue. He speaks of *Seven Pillars* as "a work seething with rancor and resentment ... firmly imprisoned in the world of practice from which its author ceaselessly proclaimed his yearning to escape." The word "practice" here means conspiracy or scheming.

Kedourie believes that the book is "impregnated with
that demonic quality which is manifest in Lawrence's
career in war and politics." *Seven Pillars* has had a hypnotic influence on many readers, a "powerful fascination."
This may be seen in the illustrations drawn by Eric Kennington for the book, "pictures of heroes and paladins,
exemplars of loyalty and chivalry. . . . But when we
compare what these men really were, the mediocrity of
some, the duplicity of others, the ordinariness of most,
with Kennington's superior beings we are repelled as by a
piece of deception which the artist not so much practiced
as, mediumlike and in the measure of his sensitivity, was
wished into practicing by a potent but impure spirit."
And what are Kedourie's grounds for calling Lawrence
an impure spirit? He quotes Lawrence himself as saying,
in his comments on Robert Graves's description of his
Arabian adventures, that he, Lawrence, "was on thin ice"
when he wrote the Damascus chapter, "and anyone who
copies me will be through it, if he is not careful. S. P. is
full of half-truth: here." The Sharifians did not capture
Damascus. Australian war records and diaries give
abundant proof that "troops of the Australian Mounted
Division entered Damascus during the night of September
30." The author of a dispatch sent from Cairo on October 8 and printed in the London *Times* of October 17,
1918, claims that the Arabs were the first troops in. This
was "most probably written by Lawrence," says Kedourie, and "displays a touch of his usual meretricious
flamboyance when it describes the incompetent ex-Otto-
man official who for a few days was head of the Sharifian
administration in Damascus as 'the senior descendant
of Saladin.' " Lawrence gives the impression "that Damascus was an Arab—was Lawrence's—conquest." The
truth appears to be that General E. H. H. Allenby for political reasons allowed the Sharifians to seem the conquerors of Damascus. The "descendant of Saladin"
opened the prisons, releasing about four thousand prisoners, among whom were murderers, robbers, opium
addicts, and forgers. These began looting and killing. The

Australian General H. G. Chauvel had to march his troops into Damascus to put down the rioters. The purpose of sending in the Arabs was to forestall the claims of the French on Syria. The "taking" of Damascus by Lawrence and Faisal is thus an invention—a piece of Hollywood history for which Lawrence wrote the scenario. He is one of those highly gifted romantic legend-makers who created "the Arab" for us; he is an early style-designer of Arab nationalism.

Kedourie is not kinder to other forms of nationalism. He has unflattering things to say of Zionism, too. He accuses the Zionists of injecting "national folklore" into Judaism.

A T Stanford, where we spend several days, exchanging the gray Chicagoland ice shield for the citrus green of Retirementland, I meet Professor Yehoshafat Harkabi (I think he is General Harkabi as well), whose specialty is the Arab-Israeli conflict. Professor Harkabi, who holds a degree from the Hebrew University in philosophy and Arabic literature, has also had a military career. From 1955 to 1959 he was chief of intelligence of the Israel Defense Forces. In Palo Alto he is a scholar doing research. The professor's face is that of a man who has spent more of his life in the sun than in the library stacks. His eyes are lighter in color than his complexion—a clear, gray gaze; his hair is grizzling; his mouth is straight, pleasant. His pleasantness is that of a single-minded and problem-burdened man. He and I are given lunch at the faculty club by an old friend of mine, Dr. Henry Kaplan, a radiologist who heads the new Stanford cancer-research laboratory. We are served large beef ribs, not enough meat on them to take our minds from the conversation.

I had already read Professor Harkabi's book *Palestinians and Israel*, written in 1974. I had also, in 1967, seen the Arab-refugee camps. They were far more squalid than the Hooverville shantytowns of our own Depression period. Those were miserable enough but they were temporary. The camps I saw in Jordan were then nearly twenty years old. It seemed to me that they were inhabitated mainly by women and children, by grannies and aged men. On the West Bank last November I passed

192

a few of these camps, now empty, the narrow shacks moldering away. Many of the refugees are employed, and resettled in towns and villages. Economic improvement has not, however, calmed the Arabs. It has, if anything, sharpened their discontent. And yet, as recently as 1972 Professor Harkabi wrote that these people of the West Bank were "preoccupied with the new opportunities for improving their standard of living," and that many were indifferent to the question of their political future and were in effect "self-depoliticized."* He intended no disparagement by this. He meant that they were busy raising their living standard and content to leave politics to the politicians—especially those in the Arab states.

This is not the situation in 1976. Reading the papers, listening to the radio, watching television, Palestinian peasants and townspeople have become aware that the attention of the world has been fastened on their political problems. True, Israel's military government has been mild, the running sores of the refugee camps in which so many thousands lived under Jordanian administration are beginning to dry and heal, but there is no settlement in sight. For Israel, the occupation is costly and embarrassing. Israel, born out of a national liberation movement, now seems to be denying the Palestinians their political liberties.

We Westerners do not understand the Arab problem, says Professor Harkabi; nor do the Israelis, unfortunately, know much about it. They had better learn what the conflict is about. Israel's leaders, if they are to meet the problem rationally and resolve it, will have to find out who the Arabs are and on what a peace must be based. Harkabi speaks quickly and without circumlocution. The Zionists did not come into Palestine with a plan to expel the Arabs. Zionism hoped to establish a Jewish state, but when Herzl failed to obtain an international charter for such a state the Zionists limited themselves

*"The Problem of the Palestinians," *Palestinians and Israel* (Jerusalem, 1974).

to the purchase of land for cultivation. This land was bought from Arabs, not taken by force. Jews had lived in Palestine continuously since ancient times. Nor did the arrival of Jewish settlers from Europe interfere with the Arab struggle for self-determination. Until recently there was no popular Arab nationalist movement and no struggle for self-determination. Of those early days—the eighteen-eighties and nineties—Harkabi writes, "The Palestinian Arabs gave little evidence of being particularly attached to the country, and many of their leaders themselves sold land, even while to the outside protesting against it." I have heard it argued, by the way, that there was a Palestinian autonomy movement before World War I.

The British as well as the Jews proposed solutions in the twenties that were rejected by extremist Arab leaders. There were riots and killings. The Jewish settlers organized defense units, which became the nucleus of their future army. "Arab intransigence forced partition and Jewish statehood," writes Harkabi. The Arabs would have nothing to do with the U.N. partition resolution; they rejected the plan for a separate Palestinian state, attacking from all sides. During the conflict, Palestinian society, which had never been strong, fell apart. "Most of the rich families" left the country. Arab leaders had also been quitting Palestine, an Arab nationalist historian, Walid al-Qamhãwi, reported.* They sought "tranquility in Egypt, Syria and Lebanon." They left "the burden of struggle and sacrifice to the workers, villagers, and middle-class. . . . These factors, the collective fear, moral disintegration, and chaos in every domain, were what displaced the Arabs from Tiberias, Haifa, Jaffa, and scores of villages." Harkabi concludes that "if the Palestinians were displaced, they mostly displaced themselves."

This sounds severe, but Harkabi does not excuse the

*Disaster and Construction in the Arab Fatherland, I, pp. 69–70, cited by Harkabi in "The Arab-Israel Conflict," Palestinians and Israel (Jerusalem, 1974).

Zionists from all responsibility. He is anything but un-
feeling toward the Arabs. Still, of Arab leaders he writes
that when they speak of a "just solution of the Palestinian question," they mean the wiping out of the Israeli
question. "Islam recognizes neither independence nor
equality for Jews." In the lingo of Arab nationalists,
Israel is "one of the most dangerous pockets of imperialist resistance against the struggle of peoples" and must be
"liquidated." A change in the Arab attitude involves
much more than diplomacy or politics. The Arab states,
whether feudal or leftist, recognize only the religion of
Islam. They tolerate Jews, Maronites, Copts, but only as
minorities under Islamic supremacy. The Fatah terrorists
have appealed to Islamic religious leaders to declare
their war against the Jews a jihad: a holy war must be
fought to establish a secular republic.

The ideal settlement from the Israeli point of view
would be reached if there were some way to soften the
indurated prejudices of centuries. But it is useless, especially during a mood of heated nationalism, to dream of
changing Arab culture or to hope for the development
of new organs. Organs of altruism are not about to burst
into growth. If the friendly European left had new hearts
to contribute, I doubt that the transplants would succeed. Harkabi quotes one of the Syrian fedayeen as saying, "I was among those who thought five years ago that
we must slaughter the Jews. But now I cannot imagine
that, if we win overnight, it will be possible for us to
slaughter them, or even one-tenth of them. I cannot conceive of it, neither as a man nor as an Arab. If so, what
do we wish to do with these Jews? . . . I think that among
many Jews, those living in Palestine, especially the Arab
Jews, there is a great desire to return to their countries
of origin, since the Zionist efforts to transform them into
a homogeneous, cohesive nation have failed. . . . We
have made the Jews think constantly for twenty years that
the sea is before them and the enemy behind, and that
there was no recourse but to fight to defend their lives."

The Palestinians, says Harkabi, form a distinct group

among the Arabs and do not feel themselves at home in the neighboring Arab countries. "Among the refugees," he writes, "a state of mind developed which stigmatized assimilation into Arab societies as an act of disloyalty." Some Palestinians resist efforts to improve living conditions in the camps lest this be taken as an admission that they have surrendered the hope of returning. Harkabi distinguishes between the older generation of refugees with their longing to recover their land and property, their idyll of the days before the disaster, and the younger generation which has replaced nostalgia with hatred and whose aim is not to recover the lost villages of their fathers but to return as conquerors and masters. This new generation, mixing Marxism with terrorism, has chosen Mao Tse-tung, Fanon, and Che Guevara as its favorite theoreticians, and its ideological preferences have won for it the sympathy and support of the European left.

The Palestinians are Pan-Arabists, but their acquaintance with the Arab states "did not always endear these states to the Palestinians, for they indeed had their fill of bitters with them," Harkabi quaintly writes. They have received some support but they have also been exploited and abused.

The opinion of Professor Malcolm H. Kerr, given in 1971 in *The Arab Cold War*, is that a "longstanding Western myth holds that the Palestine cause unites the Arab states when they are divided on all else. It would be more accurate to say that when the Arabs are in a mood to cooperate, this tends to find expression in an agreement to avoid action on Palestine, but that when they choose to quarrel, Palestine policy readily becomes a subject of dispute. The prospect that one Arab government or another may unilaterally provoke hostilities with Israel arouses fears among others for their own security, or at least for their political reputation." The armies of neighboring Arab states entered Israel in 1948 not primarily to protect the Palestinians but to prevent their rivals from expanding their territories.

We outsiders are the despair of the Arabists. We cannot free ourselves from our Western myths about the Muslim world. Even to use the term "Arab" convicts us of ignorance. The true state of things in the Middle East is difficult to explain to people who can never hope to rid themselves of their romancing habit of mind and their partisan or ideological distortions. I turned to Professor Kerr's book on the infighting between Nasser and his rivals in an effort to learn something about politics in the lands surrounding Israel. It gave me quite a turn to read Kerr's account of the struggle in 1970 between the Palestinian guerrillas and the army of Jordan's King Hussein. The Palestinian fedayeen in Amman roared around in their jeeps with loaded weapons. They behaved, writes Kerr, "like an army of occupation; they extorted financial contributions from individuals, sometimes foreigners, in their homes and in public places; they disregarded routine traffic regulations, failed to register and license their vehicles, and refused to stop at army checkpoints; they boasted about their role of destiny against Israel and belittled the worth of the army. Their very presence in Amman, far from the battlefield, seemed like a challenge to the regime." The guerrillas were not doing well against Israel's border patrols, but "with their own army, finances, social services, international diplomacy the fedayeen were building an incipient state of their own inside Jordan." The Jordanian government, after its 1967 defeat, had to accept the various Palestinian resistance groups but tried to control and contain them. Hussein wished to avoid a fight; some of the Palestinian organizations also wished to keep the peace, but an extremist minority, the Popular Front for the Liberation of Palestine, headed by Dr. George Habash, got out of hand. To Habash the governments of Saudi Arabia, Kuwait, Lebanon, and Jordan were dependent upon the United States "and, therefore, implicit collaborators with Israel." The PFLP boycotted Yasir Arafat's PLO, calling it bureaucratic and antirevolutionary. Habash and his followers began to give the struggle a more revolu-

tionary character through kidnaping, hijacking, and
anti-Jordanian propaganda. Hoping to preserve unity,
the other Palestinian groups refrained from criticism,
though they disapproved of the course the Popular Front
was taking. Inevitably, there were clashes between the
revolutionists and the Jordanian government. Elements
of Hussein's Jordanian army loathed the Palestinian guerrillas. "Over the past two years they had built up a reservoir of special resentment against the arrogant attitudes
of the Palestinians. The political tension was mixed
closely with social differences between the proud men
of tribal background, trained under the paternal eye of
the British, whose whole life and livelihood had been
based on loyal service to the Hashemite crown, and the
slick urbanites, the socially mobile, ideologically facile,
irreverent young men who led the resistance movement."
Professor Kerr sees a resemblance between these young
men and our own Yippies: it was, he says, the police of
Chicago facing the student demonstrators. The analogy
is inexact but is useful nevertheless.

In June 1970 the Popular Front guerrillas seized
hotels, took European and American hostages, and
threatened to blow up the buildings. A much-concerned
inter-Arab committee worked out an agreement in July,
after Hussein fired certain of his officers to satisfy the
demands of the PFLP. But in September the PFLP hi-
jacked four Western planes. Now, despite Nasser's pleas
for peace, Hussein could no longer avoid a fight. Since
1967, he and Nasser had been drawn together by common interests, but Hussein could have little confidence
in a friendship so transparently tactical. The Palestinians
were Nasser's clients; Hussein had been his enemy, one
of those reactionary rulers whom he had always denounced.

In mid-September the Palestinian commandos prepared for a general strike in support of their demands
for a purge of Hussein's regime which would leave the
King "with only nominal authority." This reckless Palestinian challenge was too much for Hussein and his army

officers. On September 17 the army attacked the Palestinians. "Not only fedayeen strongpoints but Palestinian population centers in general –especially the slums in the hills ringing Amman crowded with refugees—became the targets of point-blank bombardment by machine guns, mortars and artillery."

An Iraqi force of more than twenty thousand men stationed in Jordan and pledged to protect the Palestinian resistance did not intervene. A Syrian armored column did cross the border but withdrew after a few days of bloody fighting.

Hussein's Bedouins massacred some thirty-six hundred people. The Jordanian army, says Kerr, "killed more Palestinians in 1970 than Moshe Dayan's had done in 1967. The poignancy of this was not lost on Palestinians living on the West Bank under Israeli occupation. What did it foretell of the prospects for them and their aspirations if they were ever returned to Hashemite sovereignty? . . . Some refugees on the East Bank now sought to return to live under Israeli rule rather than remain exposed to the Jordanian army. Nor was the poignancy lost on Israelis, who added a stinging observation of their own. If this was how Arabs dealt with each other, they asked, what treatment was in store for the population of Israel if the Arabs ever got the upper hand?"

In the Arab world Nasser was criticized bitterly, for his friendship with Hussein made him an accomplice in the massacre. The political skills for which he was so highly praised had resulted once more in the deaths of thousands of Arabs. Assessing Nasser's career, Professor Kerr acknowledges his political ability, seeing him as "a man of remarkable personal strengths and political skills," a would-be Bismarck whose real forerunner was "perhaps in fact" Napoleon III. Napoleon also had had "great ambitions for himself and his country," had "weakened his international credit by being too shifty and conspiratorial, and had finally blustered into a test of strength in which the appearance of military prowess was no substitute for the real thing."

Nasser's aim had been to unite the Arab world, drive out its corrupt reactionary leaders, and get rid of the Jewish state, but he was balked in Yemen, defeated in the Sinai Desert, and his "political skills" produced nothing so impressive as the corpses I saw after the battle of the Sinai Desert in 1967—great numbers of them rotting, stinking, and liquefying. Remarkable personal strengths and political skills had gone wrong and these were the results. I asked myself how I would have felt if the calculations had been mine and I had been the leader responsible for this slaughter. Among the dead I already felt as if I were trying to pull away something heavy clinging and sick that had fastened itself on me. How could anyone bear the guilt for this? But probably the trade I have followed for so many years has made me naïve. Men in politics are different. News reached us in the desert that Nasser had made a gesture of resignation but that he had also organized demonstrations of loyalty. Under the weight of so many corpses, he had the presence of mind, the cleverness to make the right moves. Another man might have shot himself. Professor Kerr suggests that the disaster in Amman was more than Nasser could bear and seems to believe that this latest disgrace brought on his fatal heart attack. Egypt was too poor and weak a country to support Nasser's Bismarckian ambitions, and he himself, if Kerr is right, was not strong enough to bear the increasing burden of failure.

have heard Harkabi called a hawk but he seems to me rather better balanced than most of the people with whom I have discussed Arab-Israeli problems. Deeper, too, for the moral questions raised by this conflict are most important to him. He concedes that the Arabs have been wronged, but he insists upon the moral meaning of Israel's existence. Israel stands for something in Western history. The questions are not so simple as ideological partisans try to make them. The Zionists were not deliberately unjust, the Arabs were not guiltless. To rectify the evil as the Arabs would wish it rectified would mean the destruction of Israel. Arab refugees must be relieved and compensated, but Israel will not commit suicide for their sake. By now the Arabs see themselves returning in blood and fire, and Israel will not agree to bleed and burn. A sweeping denial of Arab grievances is, however, an obstacle to peace.

Golda Meir is sometimes accused of arguing that the Zionists had done the Arabs no injury whatever. In the London *Sunday Times* of June 15, 1969, she is quoted as saying, "It was not as though there were a Palestinian people in Palestine considering itself as a Palestinian people and we came in and threw them out and took their country away from them. They did not exist." Precisely speaking, she is right. "Palestinian" is a word given prominence recently by Arab nationalists. The Arabs always held that the Palestinian problem was a Pan-Arab problem. Palestine to them was southern Syria. At the time of the Balfour Declaration, Arab nationalists rejected the very idea of a separate Palestinian entity, insisting that the Arab lands were an indivisible whole. To Mrs. Meir this is no mere quibble. Under the influence of Arab propaganda the entire world now speaks of a "Palestinian homeland" and a "Palestinian people," and the word "Palestinian" has become a weapon. But what of the Arabs who *were* displaced in 1948? Many undoubtedly did displace themselves. When hostilities began, they fled not into exile but to familiar territory on the West Bank. Marie Syrkin, a professor at Brandeis University, writes, "Nobody enjoys seeing his property used by others even if compensation is available. But the very proximity of the abandoned neighborhood, while tantalizing, is the true measure of how little national loss the Arab from Palestine suffered. Even for so slight a cause as a new subway or urban relocation people are shifted larger distances and to stranger surroundings than the changes endured by the majority of the Arab refugees. Nasser had no qualms about dislodging whole villages for his Aswan Dam, despite the objections of the inhabitants, and the impressive ease with which the Soviet Union repeatedly shifted huge numbers of its people to further some social or political purpose is a matter of record. Only in the case of the Arabs has village patriotism been raised to a sacred cause."*

It is manifestly true that others have displaced peasants from their lands. Nevertheless, the *tu quoque* argument is insufficient, and that there were injustices must be granted. In 1967 there were more refugees—what of them?

These injustices are a torment and a threat to the Jews —they threaten to rob them of their achievement. Under Hitler the Jews were the lepers of Europe. No, they were worse than lepers. Lepers are isolated, nursed, and treated. There is no word for what the European Jews were between 1939 and 1945. After the war the survivors

*"Who Are the Palestinians?", *People and Politics in the Middle East* (New Brunswick, N.J., 1971).

fled. They were not welcomed in other countries. They went to Palestine—to Israel. They were joined there by some eight hundred thousand Jewish refugees from Arab lands, driven out by excited nationalists and revolutionists and robbed of their property. Herman Melville was not alone in expressing his horror at the desolation of the now disputed territory to which they came. Mark Twain wrote in *The Innocents Abroad*, "Palestine sits in sackcloth and ashes. Over it broods the spell of a curse that has withered its fields and fettered its energies. . . . Nazareth is forlorn; about that ford of Jordan where the host of Israel entered the Promised Land with songs of rejoicing, one finds only a squalid camp of fantastic Bedouins. . . . Palestine is desolate and unlovely. And why should it be otherwise? Can the *curse* of the Deity beautify a land? Palestine is no more of this work-day world. It is sacred to poetry and tradition—it is dream-land."

In this unlovely dreamland the Zionists planted orchards, sowed fields, and built a thriving society. There are few successes among the new states that came into existence after World War II. Israel is one of them. Lebanon, is, or was, another.

EDOURIE said in London that it was a pity the Jews had to become political. Was it necessary for them to establish a new state in one of the world's danger zones? Nationalism, he implied, was an evil the Jews did not need to add to their too painful history. He was saying, I think, that he regretted this, not that he blamed anyone. In going beyond his statement, the responsibility is my own. But it is difficult to apply reasonable propositions to the survivors of the Holocaust. To them it might have seemed that they had escaped from a deeper and madder spirit than the rest of us can know, a fury remote from the minds of learned historical explainers or from the "causes" that students of psychology and society normally deal in—a more wicked wickedness than most of us take into account in our hypotheses. Perhaps many of those who had gone through the horror of the death camps wanted to be together afterward. Their desire was to live together as Jews. Anyway, it is idle to speak of alternatives. The founding of a state was inevitable. It was a desperate, naked need that sent Jewish survivors to the Middle East. They were not working out historical problems in the abstract. They had had to face extinction.

What had the Arabs to face when these Jewish refugees arrived? "The worst fate that could befall the Arabs," writes Walter Laqueur, one of the ablest students of the Middle East, "was the partition of Palestine and minority status for some Arabs in the Jewish state." The founding of Israel was not sinless and pure, he says, but there was no way to avoid conflict, since "the basis for a compromise did not exist."* How, then, does he see the guilt of the Zionists? Their sin was that they behaved like other peoples. Nation-states have never come into existence peacefully and without injustices. At the center of every state, at its very foundation, as one writer recently put it, lies a mass of corpses. "It was the historical tragedy of Zionism," says Laqueur, "that it appeared on the international scene when there were no longer empty spaces on the world map." In time the cruelties of long-established nations become dim and are forgotten. In our own days, the sins of the powerful are seldom mentioned. The Russians have expelled Chechens, Kalmyks, Volga Germans, and others en masse from their home territories. Their problems are not discussed at the U.N. so this is where the matter stands: what others have done with a broad hand the Jews are accused of doing in a smaller way. The weaker you are, the more conspicuous your offenses; the more precarious your condition, the more hostile criticism you must expect.

Independent Arab states were created after the Allies dismantled the Ottoman Empire. It was then the hope of Lord Balfour that the Arabs, themselves newly freed from the Turks, would not begrudge the Jews one per cent of the liberated territories for the establishment of a Jewish national home. A "small notch—for it is no more geographically whatever it may be historically—that small notch in what are now Arab territories being given to the people who for all these hundreds of years have been separated from it," Balfour wrote. His mild hope has been rejected.

*A History of Zionism (New York, 1972).

THE brilliant young Israeli writer A. B. Yehoshua has shocked readers by suggesting that there is something in the Jews that arouses an insanity among other peoples. The German cruelty toward the Jews was a singular kind of madness. Yehoshua sees a similar insanity growing among the Arabs and developing in Russia. "Perhaps there is something exceptional in all our Jewishness," he writes, "in all the risk we take upon ourselves, in the fact that we live on the brink of an abyss and know how to do so. To us our Jewish nature is clear and we can feel it—but it is hard to say that the world can understand it, and by a certain kind of logic one can even justify this lack of understanding, because when you come right down to it the phenomenon of the 'Jew' is not an easy one to understand. For nations which encounter us in a certain historical situation, like the Germans and the Arabs, our very existence and the uncertainty of our nature in their eyes could provide the spark for whatever kind of insanity was afflicting them at the time." There is no need to be shocked by such speculations upon one of the grand crimes of our age—a crime such as may occur again. Rule out the possibility that a power of darkness or a spirit of evil causes this and you are obliged to think that certain of us may, without knowing how, provoke others to madness and murder.

It is this "uncertainty of our nature" that Jews have sought to overcome in Israel, surrendering "mystery" and becoming plain men—prosaic farmers, laborers, mechanics, and soldiers—partly in rejection of the character they had acquired in exile, partly to avoid emitting the spark for "whatever kind of insanity was afflicting" potential enemies. Jews who know Jewish history can't avoid seeing madness everywhere. Has anyone tried to understand why Jewish doctors have been so prominent in the development of modern psychiatry? Experience suggests that sanity is nothing stable and dependable. Hence the Israeli emphasis on normalcy. Yehoshua speaks of the "normalization" of the Jews in their own country. Had they not had to fight with the Arabs, this—the main task of Zionism—would have been achieved, he thinks.

"Why do the nations so furiously rage together, and why do the peoples imagine a vain thing?" asks Handel, quoting Scripture in *Messiah*. Well, here we are some thousands of years later, still raging, still imagining vain things. And here is Israel, now a nation among nations. The Zionists were not willing to lose their Jewishness in the lands of exile through assimilation. Assimilation did not work in any case; and what was there, in an era of decline, to assimilate oneself to? But Israeli society as a whole cannot avoid certain kinds of assimilation. While being "normalized" it is also being "politicized." A small state in perpetual crisis, it is forced to keep pace with the superpowers, to buy sophisticated arms at great cost and master them, to live in a condition of partial mobilization; it has to do business, to analyze correctly America's fiscal policies, the mood of the Congress, the powers of the American mass media. Out of pure need, for the sake of survival, it must immerse itself in American problems. Is it unfair to say that in their concern with American matters, Jews in Tel Aviv resemble Jewish New Yorkers or Chicagoans? Israel must reckon with the world, and with the madness of the world, and to a most grotesque extent. And all because the Israelis wished to lead Jewish lives in a Jewish state.

NEXT day I am in Chicagoland again. Like the Ancient Mariner driven towards the Pole:

And now there came both mist and snow,
And it grew wondrous cold:
And Ice, mast-high, came floating by,
As green as emerald.

Northward from my window I see the new Sears Tower, not emerald but slaty green in this light. It resembles a bar graph and is taller than a dozen icebergs set on end. It makes me think of Japanese transistor radios, hundreds of thousands of them, piled up and waiting for shipment.

I know how to warm my spirits in this town. I call my university colleague Morris Janowitz and make an appointment to meet him at the Eagle, a neighborhood joint. I want to talk with him about Israel. The Eagle is a storefront bar and restaurant. New Deal mementos and photographs of film stars and art works relieve its gloom. My favorite work of art is a long crescent-shaped panel salvaged from a demolished grammar school. When I was a kid, we had one of these panels in our assembly hall; the same painter must have turned them out by the dozen. It depicts the Chicago skyline of 1906. In the foreground is a mild but rather dumb-looking doll wearing a coronet. The name of this queenly person is *I Will* and she is the spirit of Chicago. In the bar is a rosy portrait of FDR as he did not look in 1932, and an

NRA eagle, and photos of old-time screen personalities. Senior patrons can identify these and feel at home.

Janowitz is community-minded and busy with ideas for improving the university and keeping the neighborhood from further deterioration. He is responsible for bringing excellent secondhand bookshops to Fifty-seventh Street. He is involved in the social planning of new housing developments. He is busy now with a new South Loop community in the old railroad yards. He knows how the police are behaving, how our local crime rates compare with those of Cambridge, Massachusetts, and New Haven, and how welfare families are doing and what black children are up to in the Chicago schools. There is nothing simple-minded about Janowitz. How to describe him: he is compact, solid; he hasn't much color but his is the pallor of a strong constitution; he has a dark lock that drops down at times toward his glasses. He reads widely, but he doesn't much care for novels and poems. He has mastered subjects it would kill me to work up. He is the author of *The Professional Soldier*, a sociological study of the military. He has written extensively on the role of the armed forces in Third World politics. He has, in addition, studied urban problems in education, crime, and welfare. He knows this huge, filthy, brilliant, and mean city. Janowitz's feeling for Chicago is one of the things that bring us together. He may not take much interest in Conrad, Tolstoi, or Stendhal but he is nevertheless, as they say in these parts, "my kind of people." I value his knowledge and his intelligence. He thinks rapidly and closely. You can't afford to daydream while he is talking. Torrentially sensible, he speaks with a slight New Jersey rasp. His last book was on the welfare state, but we are discussing Israel today. He comes of a family deeply involved in the issues of Zionism and has always been a supporter of Israel. Its fate is one of his most intense concerns.

Janowitz asks me how I assess the situation in Israel, and what I would recommend. I answer that I don't think my judgment has much value. I am simply an interested amateur—a learner. I can, however, tell him what I have heard from intelligent and experienced observers.

Many of these, I say, believe that Israel should have withdrawn from the West Bank long ago—on advantageous terms, of course. No responsible person speaks of a withdrawal that would expose Israel to military risks. But the government is desperately stuck with the occupation. Some of King Hussein's advisers now tell him he ought to reject Israel's offers to return the area. The Palestinians gave Jordan nothing but trouble. The line taken by these advisers to the King is, "We had to govern these people while others bribed them. Now let the Israelis govern, and we will do the bribing." Fortified by oil money and by world support, especially from the left, the Arab states see no need to negotiate with Israel. They plan its eventual destruction and they watch its domestic dissension and disorder with satisfaction. Then there is the problem of the ultra-Orthodox zealots who insist that to settle on the West Bank is their God-given right. The angry Arabs interpret the Rabin government's reluctance to restrain these settlers as a sign of approval or even as its covert policy. The Israeli religious nationalists do not themselves form a political group, but they have the Parliamentary support of the rightists. I have spoken with students of the Middle East who feel that nothing is more dangerous for Israel at this moment than this religious nationalism. They think it anti-Zionist, for the leaders of the Zionist movement had no religious-territorial ambitions. In America, even those who sympathize with Israel and support it see no reason the United States should be asked to sponsor this religious expansionism. On the other hand, many Israelis dread the thought that Israel may turn into an American satellite and they, in sympathizing with movements like Gush Emunim, are perhaps trying to assert their political independence. What they say, in effect, is that they will not sacrifice their independence simply because America gives them more than two billion dollars a year. Israelis are in great distress when they think it possible that the fate of their country may be decided elsewhere—in Washington, for instance. Can we blame them? America, God help us all, is not a comfortable country to rely upon. And Nixon, although he frightened us nearly to death, was after all consistently friendly to Israel. But what will the next administration do? When the election is over and Jewish votes and contributions no longer matter, who knows what proposals for settlement it may make?

Janowitz does not dismiss the possibility that a new President may be tough, even brutal. He points out, though, that it has from the first been America's policy to protect Israel. Without American approval and help Israel would never have come into existence. And the Americans have claimed, for some time now, that only they can bring peace to the Middle East. Nevertheless, this dependency is peculiarly hard to take. Between 1967 and 1973 the Israelis had felt themselves free at last from patronage. Now Rabin's most splenetic critics accuse him of turning Israel over to the Americans. They would sooner go it alone than become stooges and live on handouts; therefore they insist that they will not give an inch on the West Bank or in the Sinai. But, says Janowitz, occupation of the West Bank makes it possible for the international community to blame Israel for everything that is wrong with the Middle East; occupation strengthens the Palestinian movement; occupation costs Israel a lot of money and brings it nothing but grief. True, Israel has performed exceptionally well; the growth rate of West Bank agriculture has been very high since 1967, thanks to the Israelis, but the Arabs do not want to be governed by Israel. They insist on self-rule. Because of the Arab birth rate, annexation would be self-defeating—Arabs would quickly outnumber and outvote Jews. How would a democratic Jewish state solve the population problem?

The defense of Israel is "the paramount task of the Jewish community," says Janowitz, speaking now of the American Jewish community. But people are in an excited, jumpy state, and whenever he has spoken to groups on the problems Israel faces he has been attacked, his attackers sometimes implying that he is assisting the Arab cause. He takes these outbursts calmly enough. If you want everyone to love you, don't discuss Israeli politics. His position is that while "military force created Israel and keeps it alive, only a political settlement will insure its survival—physically and morally." He adds that "the future of the Jews rests on the intermingling of the Zionist impulse with the dilemmas of the Jews scattered throughout the world."

Unending crisis has produced "fanatical and frantic responses" within Israel. Of the paramilitary-religious settlements in the Administered Territories, he says that the religious settlers have understandable historical reasons for persisting in their attempts to establish themselves in areas densely populated by Arabs and that under reasonable conditions this would present no real problems. "But in the present circumstances they are deeply detrimental to the search for a political solution to the Arab-Israeli conflict." Israel's political leaders must oppose the further expansion of these settlements.

Orderly Janowitz next day sends me a memorandum expanding some of the points he made over lunch. "The Israelis must start to produce realistic initiatives and proposals for a peace agreement," he wrote. "They must come up with an extensive set of proposals to deal with the West Bank territories, since the West Bank represents the Palestinian aspirations." Preliminary proposals must be offered for discussion. "Some form of condominium would be one possible set of talking points. The West Bank territory, with mutual adjustments, would serve as the basis of a Palestinian state. But it would be a state that recognizes the interdependence of the contemporary world. The condominium would imply some joint agencies, such as telecommunications, transportation, currency, and various joint arrangements governing commerce and trade. There could be special arrangements with other Arab states. The crucial issue would be the guarantees of military security and the prevention of terrorism. As an initial step, there could be a joint Israeli-Jordanian constabulary force to carry out these tasks."

Negotiations at Geneva might open with such a proposal. These negotiations should begin at once. Janowitz says there is reason to believe that Russia would be interested in an agreement of this kind, though Russia would not be directly involved in peacekeeping activities. Perhaps other Arab states—Saudi Arabia, for instance—might support such a condominium. The Saudis "could be involved in the vaticanization of the non-Jewish Holy Places in Jerusalem." The matter of access to the Holy Places is as important to the Arabs as the security of the West Bank is to the Israelis.

Why would the Soviet Union be willing to consider supporting such a plan? The Soviets are afraid of another "military round," the consequences of which might be dangerous—the risk of escalation worries them greatly. "They are concerned about the spread of nuclear weapons into the Middle East," says Janowitz. "It must be Israeli policy to explore all possibilities for preventing the introduction of nuclear weapons into its arsenal. This is essential for its long-term security and for its moral position in the world community. Of course Israel may have to go nuclear, but such a step is a measure of final resort. An international organization that includes the International Atomic Energy Agency must be set up, with power to prevent the introduction of nuclear weapons into the Middle East."

Janowitz grants that some Israeli political leaders and intellectuals are convinced that another round of fighting can't be avoided and think that such an engagement would strengthen Israel and produce more favorable conditions for negotiation. He does not doubt that in another fight Israel's army would perform courageously and more effectively than in 1973. But it could not win a decisive victory. Another engagement "would produce another stalemate and another round of rearmament." The losses would be massive, the human cost enormous. Another

war "would tear the social fabric of Israel with profound
tragedy and devastation."

As for the United States, the support of Israel by its
political leaders "remains powerful and enduring, although it faces grave pressures. The support for Israel
in the U.S. military is equally strong, but that is not a
question since the U.S. military will follow the orders
of its civilian leaders. However, both U.S. political and
military leaders want Israel to face the realities of the
tension and confrontations of the moment. The United
States, not because of economic reasons but because of
the fact of the international situation, will take small steps
that can be interpreted as weakening Israel. The only
alternative is for Israel, with the support of the American
Jewish community, to begin immediately to move toward
a solution which will serve to reinforce U.S. commitments
and support to Israel."

The American Jewish community has "supplied crucial
resources to make the state of Israel possible." Its assis-
tance has in the past "had to be without specific conditions, for the Americans are far from the fighting front.
However, it has been clear almost since the establishment
of the State of Israel that its long-term political existence
could not be achieved by military force alone; given
time, the Arabs would win. A political settlement backed
by military might is required. Such a settlement involves
the solution of the Palestinian issue and the status of the
religious sites of the Old City. The American Jewish community has neglected its responsibility to assist the solution of these two issues. The resolution of these two
issues is essential to the security of Israel."

At the moment the picture is ugly, but there are posi-
tive signs. It is possible that anarchy in Lebanon may
have frightened and sobered the Syrians. "Whichever way
it goes, Israel must take the political initiative," Janowitz
says. Of course great risks are involved. The military
situation is delicate. The "internal balance in Israel is
weak and fragmented." Nevertheless, immediate action
must be taken. The infighting of the leaders will have to

stop. Political careers must be risked. This is no time to think of one's personal fortune. "In my opinion," says Janowitz, "an election is called for in Israel. Regardless of who wins, the political leaders will have to be more sober and more responsible."

In the grip of crisis and encircled by hostile states, Israel has remained consistently democratic. It isn't every country that would permit free elections in an occupied territory. But these elections are late; they should have been held long ago. The Arabs of the West Bank ought from the first to have been encouraged to create political alternatives to the PLO. There is no reason to think that they are eager in their prosperity to put themselves into the hands of extremists and terrorists. But the Israelis were not very realistic in 1967. When Janowitz visited Israel in 1970 and was taken on a tour of military installations, an Israeli general said to him as they stood together on the bank of the Suez Canal, "We expect to hold this for the next fifty years."

New states are often in trouble when the founding father dies, Janowitz observes. Ben-Gurion had the authority to control dissenting factions and impose unpopular but necessary decisions. Now there is no one. Neither is there time to beg Heaven for a successor.

I have been making what amounts to a personal Israel syllabus—the study of dozens of books and scores of documents. You are at times seduced into thinking that anything that can be studied and written up is also susceptible to reasonable adjustment. But then you remember that those who know the subject best are most pessimistic. And sometimes it comes over you that reasonable adjustment may be the remotest of possibilities. Occasionally the true nature of the subject bursts forth. I am reading an article* by David Gutmann, one of a group of professors who attended a conference on the region last summer and traveled about, being briefed by Arab and Israeli leaders and questioning them. Professor Gutmann quotes verbatim from a speech before the Syrian National Assembly by General Mustafa T'Las, the Minister of Defense. Eulogizing a war hero who had himself killed twenty-eight Israelis, the general said, "He butchered three of them with an ax and decapitated them. In other words, instead of using a gun to kill them he took a hatchet to chop their heads off. He struggled face-to-face with one of them, and throwing down his ax managed to break his neck and devour his flesh in front of his comrades. This is a special case. Need I single it out to award him the Medal of the Republic? I will grant this medal to any soldier who succeeds in killing twenty-eight Jews, and I will cover him with appreciation and honor for his bravery." Egyptian and Syrian leaders

*In the *Middle East Review*, Fall 1975.

speak of the founding of Israel as "the original sin"; is this sin so great that it justifies not only slaughter but cannibalism? Commentators and scholars—left, right, or center—speak of imperialism and socialism, of Middle Eastern nationalism—must we add cannibalism to this list of isms? Is this flesh-eating speech a scare tactic, a baring of the teeth calculated only to frighten; is it simply something like Lemuel Gulliver's gobbling joke on a cowering Lilliputian? I am inclined to think that the general meant what he said. Let us break the enemy's neck and tear his flesh with our teeth. The new nationalism has not revived what is best in Islam or, to judge by this frightful crudity, in the human soul.

In Western Europe and the United States, left-wing intellectuals continued to use the familiar Marxist-Leninist vocabulary, hoping for a radical solution and blaming the troubles of the Middle East on the rivalrous superpowers, especially on imperialist America. To Sartre it is evident that only Arab socialism can bring peace and justice, and by socialism he plainly means revolutionary socialism—the product of class struggle and of violence. I doubt that he would approve of neck-breaking or of cannibalizing one's enemies. From the far left also, Noam Chomsky warns in *Peace in the Middle East?* that Israel may become utterly dependent on capitalist America. In the chapter entitled "A Radical Perspective" he writes: "It is common these days to hear Israel described as a tool of Western imperialism. As a description this is not accurate, but as a prediction it may well be so. From the point of view of American imperial interests, such dependence will be welcomed for many reasons. Let me mention one that is rarely considered. The United States has a great need for an international enemy so that the population can be effectively mobilized, as in the past quarter-century, to support the use of American power throughout the world and the development of a form of highly militarized, highly centralized state capitalism at home. These policies naturally carry a severe social cost and require an acquiescent, passive, frightened population. Now that the cold-war consensus is eroding, American militarists welcome the threat to Israel. With supreme cynicism, they eagerly exploit the danger to Israel and argue that only the American martial spirit and American military power are capable of saving Israel from Russian-supported genocide. This campaign has been successful, even in drawing left-liberal support."

The Bolshevik slogan "The Main Enemy Is at Home," now some sixty years old, has lost none of its effectiveness. For American radicals, the main enemy has his base in Washington, whence all evils flow. But can one blame the threat of genocide or the capacity for it, the blood obsession, on "highly centralized state capitalism"? I am reluctant to believe that this "state capitalism" is as diabolical, conspiratorial, and all-powerful as Chomsky says it is. Does it need enemies abroad in order to keep us acquiescent, frightened, and passive? We are already frightened and rendered sufficiently passive by mugging, rape, and murder in our cities. Much clearer than the shadowy workings of centralized state capitalism is the fact that young men, mere boys of twelve and fourteen, carry automatic weapons in the streets of Beirut, and that they murder with perfect impunity, and that close to thirty thousand persons have been killed in Lebanon in little more than a year.

T. S. Eliot once spoke of statesmen as the foremost of the Gadarene swine. Ah, if it were only the statesmen. There are so many others in the stampede.

FACED with unappeasable hatreds and with interminable disputes, many Israelis conclude that it would be better to prepare to fight. True, the losses might be frightful, but at least liberty would be affirmed and dignity maintained. To live under the shadow of annihilation is unendurable. To become an American satellite is too galling. It would be better, these Israelis believe, to go it alone. Official support for settlements in Gaza, on the West Bank, and on the Golan Heights implies that in the government, too, American influence is being resisted. These settlements, as Terence Smith, of *The New York Times,* has pointed out, are not placed at random but form a pattern. It seems obvious that they are meant to be a permanent part of the Israeli defense system. They are not, as some claim, put there solely in order to increase the government's bargaining power. Israel evidently intends to hold on to them in an eventual peace agreement.

One of Israel's leading physicists, Yuval Ne'eman, is among those who take a strong line and argue that no ground should be given. Professor Ne'eman, until recently the defense establishment's chief scientist and principal adviser to Shimon Peres, the defense minister, resigned last winter over the signing of the interim agreement with Egypt. Ne'eman said that Israel was, in effect, duped by Henry Kissinger and that in return for its surrender of the Abu Rudeis oil fields it received a worthless piece of paper from Washington. Ne'eman accused Rabin of having misrepresented the terms of this agreement to his own Cabinet. Israel was persuaded to make unilateral concessions. "And as a result of those concessions," wrote the Jerusalem *Post,* summarizing Ne'eman's position, "Israel has now become the satellite of a U.S. whose present administration is merely feeding it bit by bit to the Arabs to ensure its own oil supply." It was unrealistic, said Ne'eman, to think of massive, long-term aid from the United States in view of the economic situation of the United States and its "atmosphere." Israel should have obtained binding political commitments from the Americans. The government had bungled. Israel yielded; the Egyptians gave up nothing. "In order to calm fears of another oil blockade and show a political success after the collapse of Vietnam, the Americans needed a Sinai agreement." The Israeli Cabinet was presented with a draft agreement, which it approved, but a new draft arrived soon afterward in which earlier promises were withdrawn. This new document, promising nothing, was not the one the Cabinet had approved. Ne'eman believes that Kissinger, like a bazaar merchant, expected the Israelis to bargain. Instead, Israel accepted the Kissinger approach, conceding everything to Egypt and postponing final arrangements with the Americans. By surrendering Abu Rudeis, Israel made itself utterly dependent on the United States for its oil. "We have lost all semblance of being a self-respecting independent state with its own national interests."

Professor Ne'eman thinks Kissinger is "a ruthless improviser who sees no more than a few months ahead." He considers peace between Israel and the Arabs "a utopian dream." The Ford administration "has written Israel off as a nuisance. It can serve one purpose, however—to be fed to the Arabs a slice or two each year, at the present stage, to increase influence and stave off an oil holdup." This is what the "step-by-step" policy means. Nor does Ne'eman expect the giveaway to stop at the pre-1967 borders. As for the Arabs, they had in 1973 the "victory" which, according to the diagnosis of the "political psychoanalysts," their self-esteem so badly needed, and they are "drunk with a sense of power. Far from being satisfied, they are now convinced that they after all have a chance to destroy Israel. Not in one grand attack but in a series of blows." Professor Ne'eman does not blame the United States, for it has a right to develop its own policies. He blames the government of Israel. Despite its strong slogans, it is inept and weak. It declared that it would never tolerate Syrian troops in Lebanon but in the early stages of civil war worked to lessen the impression that a Syrian invasion had occurred. "With our own hands we sealed the fate of Lebanon," the Jerusalem *Post* quotes him as saying. Professor Ne'eman also accuses the government of giving "the erroneous impression" that it was "saved in 1973 by the U.S. airlift. It is too late to correct this impression. But not too late to wean ourselves of the dependence on U.S. arms; and a U.S. cutoff would not be a disaster."

At this point I began to wonder whether Professor Ne'eman's views are as substantial as they are bold. Almost all my informants agree that Israel was running out of ammunition in 1973. I have always been as willing as the next writer to free myself from bondage to common sense, but despite my best efforts I haven't been able to get rid of it, quite, and common sense now asks, "If the Russians, the French, and the Americans themselves continue to supply Saudi Arabia, Egypt, and other Arab nations with sophisticated arms, how will Israel defend itself?"

Professor Ne'eman believes that Israel can go it alone. "And anyway," he says, "we cannot expect massive American aid to continue." For these reasons, he supports the Jewish settlements in Judea and Samaria on the West Bank. Ne'eman puts the next question to himself: "Don't you think you'd be bringing another war on us that way?" He replies that it is territorial concessions, rather, that will lead to war. "Giving up the West Bank would make possible a general assault which Israel *might* just be able to withstand at the cost of 50,000–100,000 killed, and which might end in another Masada on

Mount Carmel, if we were quick enough. On the other hand, standing up to the pressures raises the chances of some kind of settlement (although these are quite low). And if war did come, it would be in conditions that still permitted victory. At any rate, the question here is not one of an alternative to war. It is about an alternative to mass slaughter, of fighting a war of defense rather than mounting the gallows." Israel must be self-reliant. By ending its dependency upon the United States it may once again become a "strong ally rather than a despised satellite."

The position is this: if we do not draw the line we will be dismembered. We must forget about political settlements and rely upon our strength. I don't know how much reality there is in this—little, I suspect. But there are no smooth alternatives. All of them are full of difficulty, vexation, heartbreak.

RYING to put it all together, "to come to clarity," as one of my professors used to say. What a nice thing to come to. But this subject resists clarification. Matters like Islamic history, Israeli politics, Russian ambitions, and American problems—foreign and domestic—interpose themselves, to say nothing of Third World upheavals and the crisis of Western civilization. Instead of coming to clarity, one is infected with disorder. And I've found that talking to the public figures one reads about in the papers and books doesn't always help. My most unprofitable conversations have been with the people who presumably had most to say.

S CARCELY any point in talking with Henry Kissinger. For one thing, he doesn't want to talk. Not really. For another, he has already talked. All his views are on record and known to all the world. Everything has already been said.

The sun is shining in Washington. I am ushered into Mr. Kissinger's anterooms. I get a glimpse of what I take to be the secretary's dog, a golden retriever, and I inspect the portraits of Ben Franklin and J. Q. Adams and then the Hepplewhite and Duncan Phyfe objects in the James Monroe Room. While waiting I sip the whiskey and read the literature describing the room handed to me together with my drink by a polite attendant. Then Mr. Kissinger appears, a man with a full face and a remarkable head of hair, the tight curls mounting in dense waves, a most American sort of foreigner, speaking the language of Harvard and Washington. He leads me into his private dining room, where the waiter sets before us bowls of soup, a veal dish, and desserts too rich to be eaten. Mr. Kissinger tastes the pudding and pushes it impatiently away. He says that he can't allow me to quote him. That's all right. Everyone else quotes him superabundantly. Not only have I listened to countless discussions of Kissinger by people who know him well, but I have read Matti Golan's book and a memorandum by Martin Lipset covering Kissinger's views on Israel. The facts are coming out of my ears. Then what am I doing here? I am curious to see if I can learn what the Secretary of State feels about Israel. According to the

Lipset memorandum, Kissinger said that he didn't think his "religion" would lead him to be weak in support of Israel. His relatives had died in concentration camps and he was, of course, emotionally involved. If he had known that the Middle East situation would develop so many difficulties so soon after he became secretary, he might have refused the job. But he would certainly do whatever he could to get the best peace possible.

The secretary confronts me very earnestly, full face. His voice has dropped, and he speaks piously about his Jewish feelings. I cannot get it out of my head that a reel of tape is probably spinning under the table. He is no doubt recording this conversation, protecting himself. And why not? There is no reason he should take chances with visitors who may misquote him. It is hard to judge whether he is telling me what he most earnestly feels or what he thinks I want to hear. He says that the shadow of annihilation falls over him as it falls over other Jews, that his soul, too, is heavily burdened by fears for Israel's safety. If the world fails to rise to the moral test of preserving that safety, it will mean the end of our civilization. He represents himself as a strong defender of Israel whose efforts are not appreciated. He has given more time to the Middle East than any other Secretary of State would have given. America, which is Israel's sole support, is really more interested in the Arabs. The impression he wants to convey is that he has stood between Israel and its enemies in the American government. When he steps down, and he must step down soon, he will be missed by the very people who now assail him. Mr. Kissinger has the deftness of a master manipulator, but I feel his touch, subtle as it is. For what it may be worth, he wants to convince me of his warmth. In this warmth, however, there are icy spots—a scattering of threats which he perhaps has the habit of making when talking to American Jews: they had better understand that in letting themselves be used as lobbyists by Israel's leaders they are helping neither Israel nor themselves; in the disastrous event of Israel's defeat they too will get it in the neck. So they had better stop making so much noise in Washington and undermining their chief protector, Henry Kissinger.

Kissinger doesn't say this in so many words. He is a man of some culture (or hasn't divested himself of that appearance) and a serious student of history and politics. It is possible that he may by now have picked up the Washington big shot's contempt for the mere professor. People speak of his duplicity, coldness, cynicism, and perhaps he *is* coldly cynical and tricky. To hold his own in Nixonian Washington, a man would have to be queerly resourceful, complex, gifted in many ways— some of them disagreeable. As we talk, I recall a sentence from Golan's book. He is speaking of Kissinger's shuttle diplomacy: "The record of the discussions reveals a pattern of deception and broken promises that would have made even Kissinger's heroes, Metternich and Castlereagh, blush."

"Ah," says Mr. Kissinger, at last breaking off and looking away, "if only the Bible had been written in Uganda. Everyone would have been so much better off."

He now excuses himself, leaving me with a sense that he would prefer to go on chatting but that a dull Congressional Committee is waiting for him.

Joe Alsop, whom I also see in Washington, is one of Kissinger's most loyal supporters. Alsop doesn't want for enemies either. Many think him a mad hawk and militarist. Perhaps he is. I go to have a drink with him, not to declare my support for his views. Those have occasionally repelled me, but I have always enjoyed his company. I find his Magoo voice pleasant. His circular specs are pushed down to the end of his nose. He sits in his Georgetown library, books rising to the ceiling, sipping tea from a huge cup; he nettles his visitors now and then but he also entertains them. His reminiscences are worth listening to. He goes on too long. He refers all too often to his favorite Washington novel, Henry Adams' *Democracy*. But he does allow the subject to be changed. He is not one of the oppressive curmudgeons;

he is the picturesque kind. He argues by linking a long series of aggressive questions, punctuated by "Hey?" "Eh?" "Isn't that so—ekh?" "Has Israel better, steadier friends than me? Than Henry—eh? Where will the other fellows be when things get tough, ekh?" (He does not name these other fellows but he is speaking of supporters of Israel in the House and Senate.) "Where shall we look for them when the roll is called up yonder—ekh? ekh? Will they have the guts to be in the fight or will they take off to save their damned political skins? Tell me? Eh?" He walks about his library, a stooped but strong figure. "I'll be there when the roll is called," he tells me. "What's the matter with those Israelis? Can't they compose their damn internal differences? Do they want to be caught the way the British and French were in 1939? Fight like cornered rats? Isn't that what I try to tell them to avoid? But won't I stand by them anyway? To the last, eh? I admire those fellows. They can fight. But they don't feel friendly toward me now, do they?"

"They believe your 'Dear Amos' article was Kissinger-inspired."

"Nonsense. It's me. It's what I've thought all along, and they know it. Rabin was one of my dearest friends in Washington. Love him like a brother. But aren't those fellows too reluctant to give up ground? Buy peace with ground?"

But so far they've bought next to nothing.

ATER in the spring, the lilacs have come and gone, and blossoming trees have dropped their flowers—spring this year of 1976 is cooler than it normally is. In March I hear from friends in Israel how beautiful the season is. I remember the anemones on the hillsides of Galilee. Dennis Silk sends me some poems and writes that he is depressed by politics. He is diverting himself with a toy from Communist China; it might be of use in the marionette theater for which he writes plays. A letter from John Auerbach says he is working in the kibbutz's seaside resort taking telephone reservations, preparing for the summer holidays. About politics, he writes that he has been in Israel for thirty years now and becomes more confused by the year. The politicians fight among themselves—"all this in a hostile world, and the stack of weapons rising daily all around." There are troubles in Jerusalem over the Temple Mount, and demonstrations and riots on the West Bank. It would be a dreadful thing if such fighting were to become chronic and if, as reprisals followed killings, an Ulster situation were to develop with Jerusalem as its Belfast—Jerusalem, which Teddy Kollek has done so much to make a peaceful and a decent city.

The root of the problem is simply this—that the Arabs will not agree to the existence of Israel. Walter Laqueur writes that the issue is neither borders nor the formation of a Palestinian state.* The core of the problem is, as

*"Is Peace Possible in the Middle East," *Commentary*, March 1976, pp. 28–33.

Elie Kedourie puts it, the right of the Jews, "hitherto a subject community under Islam, to exercise political sovereignty in an area regarded as part of the Muslim domain." And Laqueur, citing Kedourie, asks, "Why ... should the Arabs, who have been unwilling for twenty-eight years to grant this right to the Jews, suddenly be willing to do so just when Arab power and influence have so greatly increased?" Nationalist movements do not renounce national territory.

A binational state would not last long, says Laqueur. In a "secular democratic Palestine," a civil war would be inevitable. And what prospects are there for a peace guaranteed by outside powers? Which powers? The United Nations? Europe? These "can be dismissed without further comment." The Soviet Union has shown little interest in ending the conflict. It has not asked the Arab "Rejection Front" to be more receptive to peace proposals. The Soviet Union "could probably torpedo any settlement not to its liking." The corollary to this is that the Soviet Union will have to be asked to approve an eventual agreement. It is not likely that the Russians would guarantee a settlement that "gives their Arab friends and clients less than they want." As for American guarantees, they are "almost equally problematical." Guarantees should provide for military intervention, and the Congress and the nation are in an isolationist mood. Even if there were a clear case of aggression, cries of "No more Vietnams" might be raised. Besides, if present trends continue, America may not be able to intervene, "because it is steadily falling behind the Soviet Union in military preparedness." The Arabs may speak of "liquidating" Israel, but as Israel has weapons of mass destruction the PLO and the Rejection Front might have to pay for such an attempt with the annihilation of their own people. "Once they realize that the only alternative to coexistence is mutual extinction a solution of the conflict will become possible," says Laqueur.

THE *New York Times* reports on May 5 a speech by former Secretary of Defense James R. Schlesinger, given at a meeting of the American Israel Public Affairs Committee. The Ford Administration, he says, is undermining moral support for Israel by putting undue pressure on it to make concessions to the Arabs. He thinks that we treat Israel as we treated South Vietnam during the 1972–73 peace negotiations, when we blamed our failure to reach a settlement on the South Vietnamese. Kissinger, during the Paris negotiations, often complained that Nguyen Van Thieu was balking his efforts to reach an agreement. "Ultimately, Mr. Thieu gave in as the result of major promises of American aid and implicit threats from President Richard M. Nixon," says the *Times*. Mr. Schlesinger speaks of "the Vietnamization of Israel in recent years." Mr. Kissinger, who bears a considerable share of the responsibility for what happened in Vietnam, asks Israel to rely on him to make its position in the Middle East secure. More, he seems to require that Israel place its faith in him alone.

What a pity it is that the great Metternich wasn't born in Uganda.

In March Laqueur wrote that Israel was standing firm but had no other strategy. For a long time now there have been no foreign policy initiatives—only reactions to moves made by others. What might Israel do? Laqueur thought it would be realistic for Israel to tell the world that it had no intention of annexing Arab territories, that it was prepared to conform with U.N. Resolution

242, which emphasizes "the inadmissibility of the acquisition of territory by war." Laqueur suggests that Israel declare itself willing to evacuate the territories by stages "over a period of five to ten years within the framework of a general peace settlement involving recognition of Israel and a regulated rectification of the 1967 borders in the interest of security." Having spelled out his recommendations, Laqueur adds that it is a long time since concrete proposals for coexistence were made to the Arabs.

But late in May I was glad to read in an article from the Chicago *Tribune* Wire Services that Ambassador Gideon Rafael in London had described Israeli proposals for peace discussions. These have not received much attention. The press was then busy with the confessions of an Ohio Congressman who put his girl friend, a talkative sexpot, on the federal payroll. When this fascinating episode in American history ends, these new proposals may reach the front page. One of them calls for a moratorium on weapons programs. The many billions of dollars saved by a disarmament agreement could be used for the resettlement of refugees and the development of the Middle East. Israel also proposes that the state of war be ended; that armed forces withdraw to secure and recognized boundaries; that a settlement of the refugee problem be negotiated; that there be free navigation of the Suez Canal and other waterways. Last is the suggestion that the big powers look on from the sidelines while the Arabs and Israelis negotiate.

These latest proposals will probably be ignored by the Arabs, but they indicate that Israel has not become immobile, inflexible, paralyzed by stubbornness of political rivals, or lacking in leadership. Its leaders are plainly still capable of pulling themselves together. Perhaps the slaughter to the north (to call it mass murder is no exaggeration) has sobered them.

No one can know what the Lebanese casualty figures are. And what if we did know? Would forty thousand dead appall us more than thirty thousand? One can only wonder how all this killing is registered in the mind and spirit of the race. It has been estimated that the Khmer Rouge has destroyed a million and a half Cambodians, apparently as part of a design for improvement and renewal. What is the meaning of such corpse-making? In ancient times the walls of captured cities in the Middle East were sometimes hung with the skins of the vanquished. That custom has died out. But the eagerness to kill for political ends—or to justify killing by such ends—is as keen now as it ever was.